TRUTH ABOUT THE

Living
Trust

THE Art OF PROPER
LEGAL PREPARATION

GREGORY P. HAWKINS, JD, AEP®

Published by Epiphany Publishing, Salt Lake City, Utah

LEGAL DISCLAIMER

Library of Congress Cataloging-in-Publication Data

Hawkins, Gregory P.
Truth about the living trust : the art of proper legal preparation / Gregory P. Hawkins.
248 pages ; 22 cm

   ISBN 978-1-942639-09-1 (hardback : alk. paper)
   ISBN 978-1-942639-07-7 (paperback : alk. paper)
   ISBN 978-1-942639-12-1 (Kindle edition)
   ISBN 978-1-942639-08-4 (ePUB edition)

   1. Living trusts—United States—Popular works.
   2. Estate planning—United States—Popular works.
   3. Trusts and trustees—United States—Popular works.
   I. Title.

KF734.H39 2025
346.7305,2—dc23

Library of Congress Control Number: 2025907307

First Edition

TRUTH ABOUT THE

Living Trust

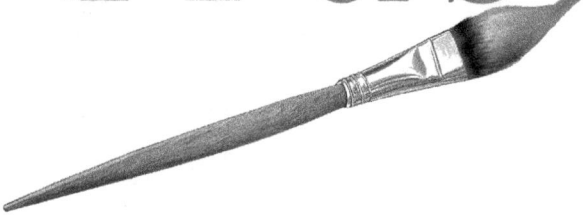

THE Art OF PROPER LEGAL PREPARATION

EPIPHANY PUBLISHING

CONTENTS

"A man who dies without adequate [preparation] should have to come back and see the mess he created."

—WILL ROGERS

" ...the fundamental purpose of estate planning is to leave a legacy for the living... The tragedy of failing to properly plan is not visited upon the dead. It is the living that suffer its unexpected and unforgiving consequences."

—*John J. Scroggin*

PREFACE

If she had only signed the papers. I cannot even remember her name. But I remember her husband's name—Fred. He was strong, intelligent and a gentle man. Kind to us and kind to those who were hurtful to him. He loved his wife with a devotion that was truly remarkable. He loved his wife's family; especially her children. He had nothing evil to say about her brother, even though he had plenty to say about him. Her brother always considered Fred an interloper who married her for her money. Ironically, she didn't really have much money. She had a pension, a small home and a few other assets. Her total estate was valued at less than $500,000. She got very sick. It was clear her time was short. Her doctor told her to get her things in order. This is when I entered the picture.

She was resolute and explicit in what she wanted to happen upon her death. She loved her children but felt each had done well to establish their own way. She made no provision for her siblings—other than to specifically mention them by name and to unequivocally declare they were not intended beneficiaries. She was wise, careful and followed counsel. She adored Fred. They had enjoyed a storybook love for nearly two decades. Because of certain peculiarities, Fred was not able to contribute much financially to their lives together. But as she had told me, he contributed much more than money ever could. She was leaving everything to Fred.

I prepared the papers. We scheduled a time to sign them. On the day appointed she was emotionally overwhelmed. Death, she said, seemed elusive, terrifying and too sorrowful to contemplate that particular day. We rescheduled. Three days later she slipped peacefully away in the night. Fred was devastated—but not as much as he would be.

Shortly after the funeral, Fred was served Court documents. He called me. He did not understand. We met. If she had only signed the papers.

Years later, many Court hearings endured, nearly $200,000 spent, family relations shredded, Fred's life completely upended, his memories of their years together no longer a storybook, the matter was resolved. If she had only signed the papers.

For me, the sad truth was that this was my professional life. Client after client; Courtroom after Courtroom; case after case. My law partner and I had effectively wielded the sword to vanquish our clients' foes and raised the metaphoric shield in their defense. It was Fred's case, or more accurately, Fred, that softened my heart and caused the scales of darkness to fall from my eyes. Although we had for many years and too many cases to remember, conquered, triumphed and thrashed our clients' antagonists, our clients had not really experienced victory.

It was not only the cost of time and money, it was the often catastrophic emotional and sometimes health tolls exacted that nearly overcame them. (No matter how well we prepared them, the time and money required always stunned them.) In litigation, every lawyer's client, win or lose, suffers. Because of Fred, I could now clearly see that the Courtroom was no place for my clients.

The purpose of a Preface in a book is for the Writer to tell the Reader why he is writing the book. I am writing this book for Fred, and, more specifically, for you. You and those you love never need to experience what Fred experienced. I have shared the message of this book with tens of thousands, face to face, and helped many thousands of families avoid Fred's experience.

Fred's experience brought my epiphany into sharp focus. Since then, I have vowed to do my best to keep my clients out of Court. This book goes a long way to deliver on that pledge.

DEDICATION

To Fred and the many others who have suffered the avoidable robbery of their families' temporal, financial, sovereign, private and emotional legacy through litigation.

"The best time to plant a tree was 20 years ago. The second best time is now."
—CHINESE PROVERB

"Failure to plan is planning to fail."
—BENJAMIN FRANKLIN

"You cannot escape the responsibility of tomorrow by evading it today."
—ABRAHAM LINCOLN

INTRODUCTION

Without proper preparation, Modern Grave Robbers will steal from your family—time, money, choice, privacy and peace.

In over 35 years of legally preparing thousands of people for death and in fighting the battles in and out of Court of those who failed to adequately prepare, I have seen just about every folly and tragedy that failure to prepare properly can bring.

The widow who spent $150,000 of her $450,000 estate in attorney's fees and over two years in court to fight off what she thought were loving family members.

The financial planner who died slowly of cancer but failed to prepare. His profession was teaching others to prepare. His wife, a second marriage, had nearly a year-long expensive battle with her own family.

The clients, almost too many to number, who decided to prepare but waited too long and tragedy struck—expensive, time-consuming, contentious tragedy.

Failure to plan is the very definition of Modern Grave Robbers. Proper planning can eliminate conflict, great expense and wasted time. Your legacy is not your money or property. Your legacy is your family and the sweet, tender connections they have. With experienced guidance, it is simple and convenient to protect that legacy.

Did you know that most, not some, but most people in this country fail to plan at all? Over half. Some studies say that as many as 69% of people fail to properly plan for the inevitable.

Here is what happens if you fail to plan properly. In many states, the State Legislature has passed laws to help cushion the pain of their citizens who fail to plan. These States have created a two-track system of Probate—Informal Probate and Formal Probate. Formal Probate requires litigation and is very expensive, contentious and time consuming.

Informal Probate is the cushion, or the help that State Legislatures have created. With Informal Probate you spend a minimum of six months in a Court-involved process. Dr. Rosemary Carlson, a professor of finance at Morehead State University, in 2023 estimated that the cost for Informal Probate ranges from 3% to 8% of the value of the estate and more if a lawyer is involved. Most find it necessary to have the aid of a lawyer. Compared to the tens of thousands needed for Formal Probate, you can see the cushion. Besides the time and the expense, Informal Probate is public and by its very process invites conflict. The process allows, even invites, just about anyone to raise questions or even make a claim. If there is a question or an issue or a problem that raises a question, that issue must be resolved by the Judge. The Informal Probate will be changed to Formal Probate and then you're off to the battle—time, money, contention.

Who must go to Probate? If you die with or without a Will and own real estate and fail to otherwise plan, Probate is required.

Here's something many people do not know. A Will cannot avoid Probate. A Will requires Probate. If a Will is used it must go to Probate. Every Will must be probated. Now you may be thinking, my aunt had a Will and we did not go to Probate. One of two things occurred.

1. You actually did go to Probate and you did not know it; you may not have been directly involved. or

2. You did not use the Will legally.

A Will cannot be used legally without Probate. A Will has no legal force or effect without Probate. Probate is required to give a Will legal effect.

If you are one of more than 60% in this country who has done nothing to prepare and you own real estate, including your home, Probate is required to pass title to that real estate to the next generation. But here is the catch: if you did nothing to prepare, then upon your death you made no choices. You did not choose who is in charge of your estate and you did not choose how your estate is distributed or divided up. If you have any special circumstances with your family, it does not matter, you made no choices. By not preparing, you made a direct invitation to Modern Grave Robbers to hurt your family.

What is the most flexible way to pass your estate to the next generation?

What is the most efficient way to pass your estate to the next generation?

What is the most cost-effective way to pass your estate to the next generation?

What is the best way to pass your estate to the next generation?

It is the Revocable Living Trust Centered Estate Plan. I have never met a lawyer, a financial planner, an accountant or other professional that was experienced in this subject matter—that of legally preparing for death—who did not agree 100% that the Trust Centered Estate Plan is the most flexible, most efficient, least expensive and the best way to legally prepare for death.

What is the Revocable Living Trust Centered Estate Plan? Whether you live in Delaware, Florida, Nebraska, California, Montana, Texas, Hawaii or anywhere in the country, the Trust Centered Estate Plan consists of six documents:

1. The Trust
2. The Pour-Over Will

3. The Durable Power of Attorney
4. The Healthcare Directive
5. The Living Will, and
6. The Deed to your real estate.

What is a Trust? A Trust is a contract recognized and effective in all fifty States and internationally. The person who sets up the Trust is called the "Settlor" sometimes referred to as the "Trustor." The IRS refers to them as the "Grantor." The other party to the Trust contract is the "Trustee." It is the Trustee who administers the Trust by following the terms of the Trust. There is a third party who is actually the focus of the Trust—the Beneficiary, the person whom the Trust was created to benefit.

Why does the Trust *not* have to go through Probate? When you are using a Trust to prepare for death, the Settlor, Trustor, Grantor of the Trust and the initial Trustee are often the same person. When that person dies the Trust stops being revocable and becomes irrevocable.

At that point, the Trust is legally considered a person, a legal entity. But the Trust does not die, so there is no Probate; there is no time-consuming legal process; there is no public process. This is not a lawyer's trick; it is the way the law is designed to work. If the Trust is artfully and skillfully written, there are often no taxes, contention, or expense to distribute the estate and close the Trust. It is flexible, efficient, very inexpensive and the best way to legally prepare for death.

There is a critical, vital and highly important aspect to the preparation of the Trust. Let me illustrate with a story.

It is an experience I had with my granddaughter Lily. Time has eroded some of the details. Lily invited me to the garage to see the painting she had created. She was seven. I looked at the painting and as with all grandfathers, I felt charmed by her efforts. But I also could not really tell what she had painted— it was kind of a mishmash. About 10 feet away, among the normal debris in the garage, was a crumpled-up print of a very nice Monet. I was struck by its beauty, its use of color, its vibrancy. I approached and looked closely. Even the brush strokes captivated me.

I looked back at Lily's painting and then to the Monet and I of course could see the difference, but Lily could not.

It's the same with the Trust. Just because Lily called her painting "art" did not make it so. Just because a document is called a "Trust" does not make it proper legal preparation that will avoid taxes, contention, expense, etc.

The worth, the value of a Trust is in its words. It must be skillfully and artfully written by an experienced lawyer who has refined its terms in the very crucible of conflict and the death of many clients. Just like an "artist" who understands that blue and red combined results in purple but may not know how to blend all

the colors together to create a masterful work of art—
it is so with many lawyers who create Trusts. They
may understand the basics but may not have been
tutored by experience and time to be able to create an
artful Trust. There are Lily-quality Trusts and there are
Monet-quality Trusts. The only way to avoid problems,
to avoid Modern Grave Robbers, is by using a Monet-
quality Trust.

Let me share with you a couple of insights that
illustrate the difference between a Monet Trust and a
Lily Trust.

The Trust must be comprehensive. Comprehensive
means it must take care of the future without knowing
what the future will be. An example: Most people do
not have heirs with a disability, who receive government
assistance. But what of the future? An accident; an
illness. One or more of their heirs may find themselves
on government assistance like Supplemental Security
Income or Medicaid. That heir will be limited in the
amount of money he or she may be able to receive—
including an inheritance. But here is what most people,
including many lawyers, do not know. In the 1990s,
Congress passed many laws benefiting people with
disabilities. One of those laws allows you to leave
an inheritance to an heir with a disability, known or
unknown, without affecting their government assistance.

The vehicle in which you must leave the inheritance
is called a Supplemental Needs Trust or a Special Needs

Trust. Most, and I mean nearly all Trusts, do not take advantage of this law benefiting people with disabilities. A Monet-quality Trust does.

Another example of a comprehensive Trust. What is to be done with a quarrelsome relative or a contentious heir or a fake heir? More than 70% of the thousands of Trusts I have reviewed do not have a basic non-contest clause. But even if they did, a basic non-contest clause only makes it more likely that you win at the end of the contest. That contest will use up substantial resources of time, money, and family harmony. A Monet-quality non-contest clause will allow you to stop the contest before it really begins.

There are probably two dozen terms written into a well-drafted Trust, a Monet-quality Trust, that takes care of the future without knowing what the future will be—that make the Trust a comprehensive Monet-quality Trust.

A Monet quality Trust will be administratively simple and convenient. It will be simple for the person setting it up and for those administering it at death. It will seldom require the need of a lawyer to administer it either before or after death. It will be convenient for your family.

A Monet-quality Trust will be cost effective. It will be affordable to set up and cost free, or nearly so, to administer upon death—certainly much less than not preparing properly.

The Trust is the most important part of the Trust Centered Estate Plan. It should be carefully, skillfully and artfully written by a lawyer with much experience in the arena that surrounds legally preparing for death. This is not a task for the novice or for a lawyer whose primary focus is not on this specific area of law.

While the Trust is the most important of the six documents making up the Trust Centered Estate Plan, the Pour-Over Will is the least important. The sole purpose of the Pour-Over Will is as a precaution. It exists only to be used if an asset is left out of the control of the Trust. For example, you purchase a new parcel of real estate but neglect to transfer it to the Trust. You die. Now that parcel must be transferred to the Trust. It is the Pour-Over Will that will be used, through Probate, to make the transfer. Remember, it is intended that the Pour-Over Will never be used—it is a precaution only.

What is the Durable Power of Attorney? A Power of Attorney is a document in which you appoint someone to act for you. If it is "durable" that person continues to act for you even if you lose the capacity to make your own decisions. Durable Powers of Attorney are powerful legal documents and can be very useful, especially when they are part of a Trust Centered Estate Plan. Durable Powers of Attorney are effective in all 50 states by statutory law. While you are still living, this document may be the most practical of the six documents. It is very helpful, even essential, if you become mentally incapacitated.

What is a Health Care Directive? A Health Care Directive allows you to appoint someone to make health care decisions for you if you are unable to communicate. A properly written Health Care Directive will avoid delay and contention at a time you want no contention or delay.

What is a Living Will? This is probably the document that appears most often in the media. The Living Will can direct physicians to stop life support that is keeping you alive if your condition is terminal. It shifts the burden of decision from healthcare providers to you. You can make this decision for yourself, in advance, for the future or you can appoint someone in whom you have confidence to make that decision at the time. This wonderful document can save great emotional stress on your family as well as untold resources.

Why is the Deed included as one of the six documents of the Trust Centered Estate Plan? All real property, all real estate, should be transferred to the Trust by properly drafted deeds. There are many types of Deeds: Warranty Deed, Special Warranty Deed, Grantor Deed, Quit Claim Deed and others. Each deed has different requirements and different consequences. Trust lawyers often use the Quit Claim Deed as the deed of choice to transfer your real property to the Trust. The Quit Claim Deed, in many circumstances, is more flexible and allows you to avoid problems. If the Deed is not properly prepared, conflict and expense will follow.

The last issue in this Introduction is what I call the "Mayflower Moving Truck Principle." This is simple. It is the idea that we have no idea at all when we will die.

"Your legacy is being written by yourself. Make the right decisions."
—GARY VAYNERCHUK

"The future depends on what you do today."
—MAHATMA GANDHI

"Estate planning is an important and everlasting gift you can give your family."
—SUZE ORMAN

CHAPTER ONE

The Trust Centered Estate Plan

In our journey we will, in some depth, discuss the individual elements and documents that make up the Trust Centered Estate Plan. We will look more deeply into the serious areas of caution, such as avoiding Probate and the folly of joint tenancy. We will discuss thoroughly the drama, the shift and improvement in estate planning by the change in Federal estate tax law that came in 2012 which made the use of the AB Trust all but obsolete. We will then discuss the critical importance of choosing the right person to be the Successor Trustee of your Trust. We will examine the Durable Power of Attorney and the crucial role of healthcare documents and their differences.

This Chapter will serve to bring these diverse elements and documents together and illustrate the benefit of the Trust Centered Estate Plan. It will begin to lay the foundation for the serious questions of what makes a Trust actually useful, effective, and even powerful; what differentiates one Trust from another; what makes it more than just words on paper. Near the conclusion of our journey we will address the question of how to choose the right lawyer to draft your Trust. We will then conclude with a principle that will help us grasp the idea that the conclusion of this book is really the beginning of your journey, not the end.

This Chapter looks into the design and purposeful structuring of estate plans that prioritize not only the seamless transition of assets but also the personal welfare and preferences of the individuals at their core.

In the realm of estate planning, where the preservation of your legacy and the well-being of loved ones are paramount, the Trust Centered Estate Plan emerges as a sophisticated strategy that transcends traditional approaches. Through an examination of Revocable Living Trusts, Pour-Over Wills, Durable Powers of Attorney, Advanced Healthcare Directives, Living Wills, and Real Estate Deeds, this Chapter illustrates the comprehensive nature of such planning. It highlights the importance of foresight, flexibility, and the careful selection of legal mechanisms that align with the individual's values and circumstances.

This Chapter invites you to consider the broader implications of estate planning, moving beyond mere asset distribution to address critical considerations of privacy, Probate avoidance and the safeguarding of personal autonomy in times of incapacity. By weaving together practical examples and theoretical insights, it aims to help you with the knowledge and encouragement needed to better understand your own Trust Centered Estate Plan. Through the examples shared of some who have navigated the complexities of estate planning, you will gain a deeper understanding of the potential challenges and rewards that come with such an endeavor.

Let us reflect on the essence of estate planning as an act of love and responsibility—a means to protect, provide for and honor our families and ourselves. The Trust Centered Estate Plan stands as a testament to the power of strategic planning and legal insight in achieving these noble goals.

In the nuanced sphere of estate management, the adoption of a Trust Centered Estate Plan represents a paradigm of strategic foresight, meticulously sculpted to ensure the seamless preservation and transfer of one's legacy, safeguarding both family welfare and the fruits of a lifetime's labor. This comprehensive strategy, underpinned by the symbiotic relationship between Revocable Living Trusts, Pour-Over Wills, Durable Powers of Attorney, Advanced Healthcare Directives, Living Wills, and Real Property Deeds, embodies a holistic approach to estate planning. It not only addresses asset distribution but also encapsulates considerations of personal welfare, family dynamics and legal protections.

Revocable Living Trust: The Architectural Blueprint of Estate Planning

At the vanguard of this planning strategy the Revocable Living Trust serves as an architectural blueprint, offering a framework that transcends the conventional limitations of Will-based estate plans. This instrument facilitates a preemptive transfer of assets into a Trust, granting individuals stewardship over their estate throughout their lifetime and assuring a direct, Probate-free transfer to Beneficiaries thereafter. This strategic mechanism not only maintains the Grantor's dominion over their assets; including, the flexibility to amend the Trust as personal circumstances evolve but also guarantees privacy and financial efficiency by obviating the public and often protracted Probate process.

Pour-Over Will: The Universal Safety Net

Operating in tandem with the Trust, the Pour-Over Will acts as a universal safety net, meticulously designed to capture any assets inadvertently left outside the Trust's domain at the Grantor's demise. This instrument channels such assets into the Trust, ensuring a comprehensive and unified asset distribution in strict accordance with the Grantor's wishes, thereby leaving no asset unaccounted for.

Durable Powers of Attorney: The Pillars of Continuity

Embedded within the estate plan, Durable Powers of Attorney for financial decisions stand as a pillar of continuity, safeguarding the Grantor's interests during unforeseen incapacitation. These legal provisions delegate decision-making to trusted agents, mirroring the Grantor's predetermined directives, thus providing stability and reassurance to both the individual and their family in tumultuous times.

Advanced Healthcare Directive and Living Will: The Manifesto of Care Preferences

The Advanced Healthcare Directive, often integrated with a Living Will, articulates a clear manifesto of the Grantor's medical treatment preferences. This declaration is pivotal, ensuring that healthcare decisions are reflective of the Grantor's wishes, thereby mitigating the emotional and logistical burdens on family members during critical moments.

Real Property Deed: Properly Placing Your Most Valuable Asset in the Trust

Real estate is transferred from party to party by a Deed. Choosing the proper deed and correctly vesting title in the Trust is critical. If incorrectly done, the resulting complications may take expensive Court involvement to remedy.

Privacy, Probate Avoidance, and Asset Safeguarding

The Trust Centered Estate Plan excels in its capacity to preserve family privacy and expedite asset transition without Probate. By mitigating public exposure and circumventing potential creditor claims, this planning ensures asset preservation for its designated heirs, enhancing the efficiency of the distribution process while concurrently fortifying the estate against external claims.

Flexibility and Control

Trusts are lauded for their unparalleled flexibility and control over asset distribution, enabling the crafting of legal solutions tailored to the unique needs of Beneficiaries. This adaptability facilitates the imposition of inheritance conditions, provisions for individuals with special needs and the safeguarding of assets for future generations, epitomizing the Trust's foresight and versatility.

The Strategic Imperative

The Trust Centered Estate Plan is emblematic of a strategic imperative, designed not merely to secure one's legacy but to instill a sense of peace, knowing that both personal and familial futures are comprehensively protected. It underscores a commitment to meticulous planning, ensuring that each component harmonizes to protect the Grantor's assets, honor their healthcare directives and safeguard their family's future. Engaging with an experienced estate planning attorney is paramount in navigating this complex landscape, ensuring the plan resonates with the Grantor's aspirations and values. Through the strategic use of Trusts, individuals can fortify their families against the uncertainties of the future, ensuring their legacy's endurance for generations.

In essence, the Trust Centered Estate Plan is a strategic framework that not only secures your legacy but also grants you peace of mind, knowing that your wishes will be honored. To craft a plan that aligns with your goals and values, consulting with an experienced estate planning attorney is essential. By embracing the power of the Trust, you can protect your family from Modern Grave Robbers who will take from your family time, money, choice, privacy, and peace.

Clara, a dedicated mother and successful business owner, understood the importance of planning for the future. Concerned about ensuring her children's financial security and avoiding the complexities of Probate, Clara decided to create a Trust Centered Estate Plan centered in a Revocable Living Trust. By transferring her assets into the Trust, Clara maintained control over her wealth during her lifetime and established a clear roadmap for asset distribution upon her passing.

When Clara suddenly passed away from a heart attack, her family was devastated but found solace in the meticulous estate plan she had put in place. Thanks to the Revocable Living Trust, Clara's assets seamlessly passed to her children without the need for Probate, without conflict and without taxes, saving time and minimizing the emotional burden on her loved ones. Clara's experience exemplifies the power of a Trust Centered Estate Plan in preserving family harmony and ensuring a smooth transfer of wealth across generations.

James, a retired veteran with a passion for travel, never anticipated the challenges that would arise when he suffered a stroke during a trip abroad. Suddenly incapacitated and unable to make decisions for himself, James found himself in a vulnerable position until his daughter, June, stepped in as his designated Attorney in Fact for healthcare. With a Trust Centered Estate Plan that included comprehensive Advance Healthcare Directive, James had appointed June to make critical healthcare decisions on his behalf, ensuring that his wishes were respected even in times of crisis.

June's quick action and adherence to her father's wishes not only saved James's life but also preserved his dignity and autonomy during a challenging period. James's experience highlights the importance of an Advanced Healthcare Directive in a Trust Centered Estate Plan. It provides a safety net and protection in times of incapacity. It ensures that one's values and preferences are the guide for decision making.

In a tale of family intrigue and unexpected twists, the Edwards family navigated the complexities of estate planning after the sudden passing of their father, Henry. With a Trust Centered Estate Plan in place that prioritized privacy and Probate avoidance, the family was able to shield their personal affairs from public scrutiny and maintain confidentiality during a challenging time.

As the family gathered to mourn and honor Henry's legacy, they were relieved to find that the details of his estate remained private, thanks to the Trust structure he had established. By avoiding Probate, the Edwards family not only preserved their privacy but also expedited the distribution of assets, allowing them to focus on honoring their beloved father's memory and supporting one another through the grieving process.

These experiences illustrate the legal and practical principles of the Trust Centered Estate Plan and help us understand the transformative impact of strategic planning and thoughtful preparation. By incorporating the Revocable Trust, Pour-Over Wills, Durable Powers of Attorney, Advance Healthcare Directives and Living Wills, and emphasizing privacy, flexibility, and asset protection, you can create a robust estate plan that safeguards your assets and preserves your legacy for future generations.

The experiences of Clara, James, and the Edwards family illustrate the tangible benefits and peace of mind that come from thoughtful estate planning. Clara's foresight ensured her children's financial security and sidestepped Probate complexities. James's predicament highlighted the indispensable value of having Advance Healthcare Directives ensuring his healthcare wishes were honored. The Edwards family's experience underscored the importance of privacy and Probate avoidance, showcasing how the Trust Centered Estate Plan can protect the personal affairs of a family in times of sorrow.

These examples underscore the essence of estate planning as an act of love, responsibility and foresight—a means to not only safeguard assets but also to honor and protect one's family. The Trust Centered Estate Plan, with its strategic incorporation of key legal instruments, stands as a testament to the power of proactive planning and legal insight in achieving these noble objectives.

In essence, this Chapter is an invitation to recognize and embrace the power of strategic estate planning. By doing so, individuals can ensure that their legacy endures, protected from the uncertainties of the future and preserved for the benefit of generations to come. The Trust Centered Estate Plan is not merely a legal strategy but a profound expression of care, ensuring that one's final wishes are honored and that their family is shielded from unnecessary hardship.

"To be prepared is half the victory."
—MIGUEL DE CERVANTES

"When preparation is lacking, it's not just your failure but a failure shared by all those depending on you."
—STEPHEN R. COVEY

"It is better to look ahead and prepare than to look back and regret."
—JACKIE JOYNER-KERSEE

CHAPTER TWO

Building a Fortress of Protection

In the realm of estate planning, there exists a powerful shield that can protect your family from the grasp of Modern Grave Robbers—the Trust Centered Estate Plan. When created with care, precision, and experience, the Trust Centered Estate Plan can fortify your legacy and ensure that your loved ones are protected from the devastating effects of inadequate planning. Truth About the Living Trust unveils the five ways Modern Grave Robbers can hurt your family—by stealing time, money, choice, privacy, and peace. In this Chapter, we look into the heart of why one must properly and legally prepare for death.

The Imperative of Proper Preparation

At the core of estate planning lies a fundamental truth—death is an inevitable part of life. Over 9,000 people die every day in the United States, which means nearly fifty people will pass while you read this chapter.

Contemplating our mortality may be a daunting task, yet it is essential to recognize the profound impact that a lack of preparation can have on our loved ones. Proper and legal preparation for death serves as a fortress against chaos, ensuring that your wishes are honored, your assets are protected and your family is provided for in the event of your passing.

Estate planning is not merely a matter of drafting documents and allocating assets. It is a complex legal tapestry woven with intricate threads of statutes, regulations and case law. To navigate this intricate landscape effectively, one must engage in thorough legal analysis to ensure that the estate plan withstands the test of time and legal scrutiny. By understanding the nuances of estate planning laws and regulations, individuals can craft a comprehensive plan that safeguards their legacy and shields their family from harm. To illustrate the significance of proper estate planning, let's take a brief peek into the lives of individuals whose lack of preparation led to devastating consequences.

Sarah and David, a loving couple with two young children, had always intended to prepare for future tragedy by creating a comprehensive estate plan. However, their busy lives and reluctance to confront their mortality led them to procrastinate this crucial task. Tragedy did strike. David was killed in a car accident leaving Sarah and their children vulnerable. David and Sarah never thought that he would be one of those that are killed in a car accident every twelve minutes. Who would have considered such a thing? Without proper planning, Sarah found herself embroiled in a lengthy legal battle over David's assets, enduring emotional turmoil and financial strain.

The Smith family, once united by love and shared dreams, found themselves torn apart by a bitter dispute over their patriarch's estate. Franklin Smith, a successful entrepreneur, had amassed a considerable fortune over the years. If it is not ironic enough that this careful planner failed to plan, consider this. Franklin knew he was dying. He had terminal cancer. One person every twenty seconds dies of cancer in this country—every twenty seconds. Franklin had plenty of notice. His failure to establish a clear estate plan sowed the seeds of discord among his heirs. With no guidance on asset distribution or inheritance wishes, the Smith family descended into chaos, with siblings pitted against each other in legal battles that eroded not only their wealth but also their familial bonds. The legacy that Franklin had worked so hard to build crumbled before his family's eyes, underscoring the profound impact of inadequate estate planning. They learned by very sad experience that their father's legacy was not his wealth and property but rather, the tender bonds of family.

Contrasting the tales of Sarah and David, and of the Smith family is the story of the Grace family.

Helen Grace, a meticulous planner and devoted mother, took proactive steps to ensure that her family's future was secure. Helen was conscientious about her diet, exercise, and general health. But she knew and paid attention to the statistics. For example, unexpected home accidents take someone every 3 minutes and 21 seconds; unexpected cardiac events claim a life every forty seconds. By working closely with expert estate planning lawyers, Helen established a comprehensive Trust that ensured her wishes regarding asset distribution, guardianship of her children and other vital aspects of critical preparation were followed without legal conflict or administrative complexity. When tragedy struck and Helen passed away unexpectedly, her family was protected from the turmoil that often accompanies such events. The Trust she had had meticulously crafted by experienced professionals served as a beacon of stability, guiding her loved ones through their grief and ensuring that her legacy endured with love and dignity.

The Johnson family, spanning three generations of entrepreneurs and visionaries, exemplifies the power of proper estate planning in preserving generational wealth. Starting with Samuel Johnson who founded a successful business empire. Each member of the Johnson family understood the importance of creating a solid estate plan to protect their assets and ensure a smooth transition of wealth to the next generation. Through the use of well-crafted Trust Centered Estate Plans and strategic tax planning, the Johnson family not only secured their financial legacy but also instilled a sense of responsibility and stewardship in their heirs. The legacy of generational wealth they built stands as a testament to the enduring impact of proper legal planning and foresight.

The stories of Sarah and David, the Smith family, the Grace family and the Johnson family, remind us of the fragility of life and the importance of preparing for the inevitable. The list of well-known people who have died without timely and thorough preparation is extensive; from Prince to Aretha Franklin, from Howard Hughes to James Gandolfini; from Abraham Lincoln to Pablo Picasso. The emotional trauma and economic loss serve as a stark reminder of the importance of timely and thorough estate planning. "Timely," of course, is not entirely in your hands. Procrastination due to busyness, apathy, fear, lack of understanding, or the very common but unspoken belief that death is not in your immediate future, invites trouble. "Thorough," on the other hand, eludes nearly everyone—even lawyers. Expert estate planning requires not merely training, but a great deal of focused experience. Not every lawyer who you may engage to help you is equipped to adequately do so, as we will discover in this book. Not to worry, there are many well-trained and experienced lawyers available to help you thoroughly prepare. Proper and legal preparation for death is not merely a task to check off a list; it is a profound act of love and responsibility towards those we hold dear. By creating a well-considered and properly drafted Trust as a fortress, we can ensure the protection of our family. The imperative of proper and legal preparation for death cannot be overstated. Through thorough and proper estate planning, we can ensure that our legacy endures, and our family is safeguarded for generations to come.

"He who has a Will, plants a fruit tree in the garden of a lawyer."

—ITALIAN PROVERB

"Where there is a Will, there is a lawsuit."

—ADDISON MIZNER

"The postmortem squabblings and contests... have made a Will the least secure of all human dealings."

—LLOYD V. WAYNE CIRCUIT JUDGE
23 N.W. 29, 30 (MICH. 1805)

CHAPTER THREE

The Will Dilemma

In the landscape of estate planning, the Will stands as a traditional yet complex instrument used to outline one's final wishes and distribute assets upon death. While the Will serves as a foundational document in the legal preparation for death, its use comes with a myriad of practical, family, and legal risks and difficulties. In this Chapter we will discuss the wisdom of using a Will in estate planning and explore the challenges and consequences that individuals may face when relying solely on this document to protect their family.

The Will, often referred to as the Last Will and Testament, is a legal document that allows an individual (the Testator) to express their wishes regarding the distribution of assets, appointment of guardians for minor children and other important matters upon death. Through the Will, the Testator seeks to ensure that loved ones are provided for and that the estate is settled as intended. While the Will serves as a valuable tool of testamentary intent, its limitations and potential risks must be carefully considered.

One of the primary practical risks of relying solely on a Will for estate planning is the potential for delays and complications in the Probate process. Probate is the legal process through which a Will is validated, assets are distributed and debts are settled. In today's litigious world the Probate process can be lengthy, costly and subject to Court oversight. For a Will to have any legal force or effect, it must go through the Probate process. Probate is to a Will what power is to a car. Without power the car does not move; without Probate the Will has no legal efficacy. Additionally the lack of flexibility in a Will may lead to unintended consequences as changes in circumstances or relationships may not be adequately addressed in the document.

The use of a Will to legally prepare for death can also give rise to family tensions and emotional challenges. In cases where family members feel slighted or excluded from the distribution of assets, disputes and conflicts may arise leading to fractured relationships and costly legal battles. Moreover the lack of clear communication and precision in the Will may leave loved ones feeling confused, hurt or resentful, further exacerbating the emotional toll of the estate administrative process.

From a legal perspective, relying solely on a Will for

estate planning exposes individuals to various risks and vulnerabilities. The validity of a Will may be challenged on grounds of undue influence, lack of capacity or improper execution, leading to protracted litigation and uncertainty regarding the distribution of assets. Moreover, the public nature of Probate proceedings can compromise the privacy of the Testator and their family, exposing sensitive information to scrutiny and potential exploitation.

It is this aspect of relying on a Will as your primary vehicle for preparation that is the gateway to many hidden crocodiles—it is public. Probate, by its very nature, is open to the public. Not merely because anyone can literally look at every aspect of the Court documents but more importantly almost anyone can legally enter into the Probate by raising a claim, a factual or legal question, or some kind of interest in the estate. If such a thing must be resolved by the Judge, the expense of time and money and emotion exponentially increases. The public nature of Probate is like a petri dish in which the worst in human nature can come to life like fungus. It nearly defies reason that anyone would purposefully plan to expose their family to the risks of Probate.

To illustrate the practical, family and legal risks of using a Will for estate planning, let us catch a glimpse at the lives of some who faced challenges and complexities in their journey towards preparing for death.

Emily and James, a devoted couple with three

children, believed that their Will adequately addressed their estate planning needs. However, when James unexpectedly passed away, Emily discovered that their Will did not account for changes in their financial situation and failed to provide clear guidance on asset distribution. For example, Emily was not fully informed of the full breadth and depth of their financial circumstances—where their accounts and investments were held, to whom they owed money, even the extent of their debt or the character of their creditors. As a result, Emily found herself entangled in a lengthy Probate process, grappling with uncertainty and financial strain. The emotional trauma may have been worse than the actual litigation. The lack of foresight and comprehensive planning in their Will led to unintended consequences. Emily and James should have had more frequent and open conversations about the details of their financial lives. They should have sought the help of experienced financial and estate planning professionals.

Their worst mistake: Emily and James have nine children. Having the children was not their mistake. What if both of them had perished? What if Emily dies before she corrects their poor planning? No one should be so foolish as to purposely saddle their beloved children with control of significant financial resources at the unseasoned age of eighteen. But that is exactly what would happen if Emily does not wrestle properly and soon with this critical issue.

The Thompson family, once united by love and shared memories, found themselves torn apart by a bitter dispute over their father's Will. Richard Thompson, a successful businessman, thought he had meticulously crafted his Will to distribute his assets among his children and grandchildren. However, ambiguities in the document and differing interpretations among family members sparked a legal battle that eroded confidence and fractured family bonds. Two of his children were named as co-executors. They were both capable, cooperative, and honest—while the father was alive. Soon after his death and in the middle of their Probate duties, they found that they did not agree on most everything. There was no practical resolution, let alone a legal resolution, except returning to Court time and time again to resolve the issues. By the conclusion of the Probate they and their individual families barely spoke to each other. This was now their father's legacy— generational animosity. The legacy of conflict that ensued from poor planning serves as a cautionary tale of the risks inherent in relying solely on a Will for estate planning. Clarity, precision and experienced legal counsel have a direct impact in preserving family harmony.

Contrasting the tales of Emily and James and the Thompson family is the story of the Carter family. Julie Carter, a proactive and forward-thinking woman, engaged in comprehensive estate planning to protect her family's future. By creating a Trust Centered Estate Plan with comprehensive provisions Julie ensured that her wishes were honored and her loved ones were provided for in the event of her passing. Julie understood that no one can predict the future. She sought out a lawyer with extensive training and expertise. He helped her to understand that comprehensive documents would provide for whatever the future brings. When tragedy struck and Julie passed away, her family was protected from the turmoil and uncertainty that often accompanies the loss of a loved one. The carefully written documents provided privacy, eliminating the unwelcome attention of potential adversaries. Other provisions provided flexibility and alternatives as the circumstances of her family changed. The peace and stability that Julie's careful planning afforded her family serve as a beacon of hope, underscoring the transformative power of proper estate planning.

When Julie asked how that was possible, the lawyer explained that through years of experience and helping many clients, a seasoned lawyer will have seen and weathered the multitudinous variables that life and death bring. Further, the work prepared for previous clients has been tested and refined in the very crucible of those clients having had to rely on the lawyer's work in death.

Emily and James, the Thompson family, and the Carter family remind us of the intricate web of challenges and risks inherent in relying solely on a Will for estate planning. The Will, while a powerful tool of testamentary intent, must be approached with care and consideration to mitigate practical, family, and legal risks. By engaging in thorough legal analysis, regular review of estate planning documents and open communication with experienced estate planning lawyers, you can navigate the complexities of the estate planning process with confidence and clarity.

So what is the "Will dilemma?" A dilemma is a situation requiring one to choose one of two or more undesirable choices. The Will dilemma is not as much about choosing between undesirable choices but more about not really understanding your choices. Sure, not planning is a foolish and undesirable choice. As we have seen relying on a Will as your primary document to prepare is fraught with risks and problems and is really not planning well at all. Two choices—both undesirable. But these are not your only choices.

By the end of this book, you will better understand that proper legal preparation is the choice that will protect your family and bring you peace. Relying on a Trust Centered Estate Plan will preserve your legacy of the sweet, tender family bonds. Before we explore that further, we need to look a bit more closely at Probate and other solutions that promise protection, but do not deliver.

"Litigation [Probate]: A machine which you go into as a pig and come out of as a sausage."
—AMBROSE BIERCE

"If you can avoid it, never mess with a lawsuit. It's a business where the profits are doubtful, the expense is certain, and the experience is bitter."
—UNKNOWN

CHAPTER FOUR

The Pitfalls of Probate

As we have seen in the previous Chapter, the specter of Probate looms as a daunting and costly process that can erode your legacy. Probate, the legal procedure through which a deceased person's assets are distributed and debts settled, carries with it a host of practical, family, financial and legal risks and difficulties. In this Chapter, we look at the complexities of Probate, touching on the challenges it presents and why individuals should strive to avoid this arduous path in safeguarding their family's future.

Probate, a Court-supervised process, serves as the mechanism through which a deceased person's assets are identified, valued, and distributed according to their Will or according to State laws if no Will exists. While intended to ensure the orderly transfer of assets and resolution of debts, Probate can become a protracted and costly ordeal that drains resources and encourages family discord. Understanding Probate and its potential pitfalls is essential for individuals seeking to protect their estate and loved ones from unnecessary hardship.

One of the evils of Probate is the time-consuming nature of the process. All Probate carries the risk of litigation. All litigation is protracted—lasting longer than you thought it would or wanted it to last. Probate proceedings can stretch on for months or even years, delaying the distribution of assets to Beneficiaries and causing financial strain on the estate and on your family. But worse, much worse than this, is the emotional strain that is inherent in all litigation. The Court oversight and required formalities in Probate can also lead to increased administrative burdens and legal fees, further depleting the estate's resources. In our modern world, no one enters the arena of litigation without a lawyer. All lawyers are expensive. Additionally, the public nature of Probate exposes sensitive financial information to scrutiny, compromising the privacy of the deceased and their family. The public nature of Probate was discussed in the previous Chapter. Please understand it is the public aspect of Probate that most often leads, if not outright invites, litigation.

The Probate process can give rise to family tensions and emotional turmoil, as family members navigate the complexities of estate settlement during a time of grief and loss. Disputes over asset distribution, challenges to the validity of the Will and disagreements among Beneficiaries can escalate into bitter conflicts that strain relationships and fracture family bonds. Hidden or buried emotional wounds from days gone by often become exposed and lead to or even ignite conflicts. The lack of clear communication and guidance in the Probate process may leave loved ones feeling confused, resentful and disenfranchised, heightening the emotional toll of navigating the legal maze of estate settlement.

From a financial standpoint, Probate poses significant risks to the estate and its Beneficiaries. The costs associated with legal fees, accountant fees, Court expenses, appraisals and executor fees can quickly deplete the estate's assets, leaving less for distribution to heirs. (In one recent case, the amount of the estate that was at issue was $1,000,000. The legal fees, just for one side of the controversy, were $1,500,000.) Moreover, the delays inherent in the Probate process may hinder the timely resolution of debts and obligations, leading to creditor claims that erode the estate's value. In cases where the deceased had complex financial holdings or business interests, Probate can expose the estate to additional risks and uncertainties, further complicating the settlement process.

Let's explore the lives of individuals who have grappled with the challenges and complexities of estate settlement through this arduous process.

The Hansen family, reeling from the sudden loss of their father, found themselves ensnared in a prolonged

Probate process that tested their resolve and unity. Despite the estate having a valid Will in place, the intricate legal requirements of Probate and Court delays prolonged the distribution of assets, leaving the family in financial uncertainty and emotional distress. The process began convivially enough. But soon the delays exposed the hidden interests of many in the family that competed with the interests of others. They soon discovered that although the Court had appointed a sibling as the executor, it was easy enough for their lawyer to pursue their own competing interest which complicated the process and created more delays. The burden of Probate weighed heavily on the Hansens, straining their relationships and draining their resources. The Probate process was just too easy to influence, exploit and manipulate. What a sad shadow to cast on a family already grappling with loss.

John, a successful businessman who owned several sporting goods stores, neglected to engage in proper estate planning, assuming that Probate would suffice to settle his affairs. He, in fact, did nothing to prepare— not even a Will. (Over sixty percent of people choose the same path as this.) However, upon his passing, the complexities of his estate and the lack of clear directives led to protracted Probate litigation, a battle that consumed his assets and fractured his family. His family had not been directly involved in his business. Each of his partners had their own interest to protect and their separate perspectives to pursue. This scenario is played out in Probate Courts every single day across this country—over and over again. The financial drain and legal entanglements that ensued left John's heirs, his partners, even his creditors, with a fraction of what they had expected and rightly deserved.

In contrast to the tales of the Hansen family and John, the Harboughs embarked on a journey of redemption by establishing a Trust Centered Estate Plan to protect their family from the pitfalls of Probate. Through careful estate planning and proactive measures, the Harboughs ensured that their assets would entirely bypass the Probate process, safeguarding their legacy of the sweet, tender family bonds and provide for their loved ones with clarity and efficiency. When tragedy struck and the head of the Harbough family died, the Trust they had established served as a beacon of stability, guiding their heirs through the settlement process with grace and dignity. The peace and security that the Trust afforded the Harbough family stood as a testament to the wisdom of avoiding Probate through strategic planning and foresight.

As we reflect on the stories of the Hansen family, John, and the Harboughs, we are reminded of the myriad risks and difficulties inherent in the Probate process and the transformative impact of proactive estate planning. The pitfalls of Probate, from practical delays to family discord, financial drain and legal vulnerabilities, underscore the importance of avoiding this foolish and arduous path. By embracing the flexible, efficient and much less expensive strategy of the Trust Centered Estate Plan, individuals can navigate the complexities of estate settlement with confidence and peace. No one voluntarily subjects their family to Probate when other options are available.

The Trust Centered Estate Plan is the other option available as a powerful and flexible estate planning tool that offers individuals a safe, efficient and powerful alternative to the Probate process. By transferring assets into a Trust during their lifetime, individuals can avoid the delays, costs and public scrutiny associated with Probate, ensuring a seamless transition of assets to their Beneficiaries upon death. The Trust allows for privacy, flexibility and efficient asset distribution, shielding families from the turmoil and uncertainty that often accompanies the settlement of an estate through Probate.

Once educated in the risks and difficulties posed by Probate, families are quick to embrace comprehensive estate planning strategies that prioritize the avoidance of this cumbersome process. By engaging in proactive planning, regular review of estate documents and open communication with skilled and experienced legal counsel, you can create a solid foundation for your family's future and ensure that your final wishes are honored with exactness, compassion and intelligence.

"*Advice is like mushrooms; the wrong kind can prove fatal.*"

—PROVERB

"*Life presents many choices, the choices we make determine our future.*"

—CATHERINE PULSIFER

"*Learning without thought is labor lost; thought without learning is perilous*"

—CONFUCIOUS

CHAPTER FIVE

The Perils of Joint Tenancy in Real Property Succession

In the realm of estate planning, the transfer of real property from one generation to the next holds profound significance for preserving family wealth and legacy. Joint tenancy, a common method of property ownership, can serve as a double-edged sword when utilized as a vehicle for intergenerational wealth transfer. This Chapter looks at the complexities of joint tenancy in the context of passing real property to the next generation, focusing on the critical implications of losing the step-up in basis and facing substantial Capital Gains tax liabilities. The stepped-up basis is an adjustment of the cost basis of inherited property to its fair market value at the time of the original owner's death. This adjustment can significantly reduce Capital Gains taxes when the property is sold by the heirs.

Joint tenancy, a form of property ownership that allows multiple individuals to hold equal shares in a property with rights of survivorship, is often chosen as a method to pass real property to the next generation. "Rights of Survivorship" means that if one of the property owners dies, their ownership automatically passes to the other property owner. While joint tenancy offers the advantage of seamless transfer of ownership upon the death of a joint tenant, it also comes with inherent risks related to the loss of the step-up in basis and potential Capital Gains tax liabilities for the Beneficiaries. Understanding the nuances of joint tenancy and its implications for generational wealth transfer is essential for making informed decisions in estate planning.

One of the most significant drawbacks of transferring real property through joint tenancy is the loss of the step-up in basis that Beneficiaries would otherwise receive in other forms of inheritance, such as through a Trust. When property is passed through joint tenancy, the surviving joint tenant(s) do not benefit from a stepped-up basis to the fair market value of the property at the time of the original owner's death. This absence of a stepped-up basis can have far-reaching implications for the Beneficiaries, as they may face higher Capital Gains tax liabilities when selling the property based on the original owner's lower cost basis.

The looming specter of Capital Gains taxes presents a significant financial challenge for families inheriting real property through joint tenancy. Without the benefit of a stepped-up basis, Beneficiaries are required to calculate Capital Gains taxes based on the original owner's purchase cost, potentially resulting in substantial tax obligations upon the sale of the property. The burden of Capital Gains taxes can diminish the value of the inherited property, limit the Beneficiaries' ability to maximize their returns and pose a significant obstacle to preserving family wealth across generations.

To illustrate the real-world impact of losing the step-up in basis and facing Capital Gains tax liabilities in real property succession through joint tenancy, let's explore the experiences of some who have grappled with the financial ramifications of joint tenancy as a method of transferring real estate to the next generation.

The Owens children, who inherited their family home through joint tenancy with their father, found themselves facing a harsh reality when the original property owner died. Despite the hopes of passing the property to the next generation, the absence of a stepped-up basis meant that the children would be liable for significant Capital Gains taxes upon the sale of the home. The burden of taxation threatened to erode the value of the father's legacy and strained family relationships as they navigated the complexities of estate settlement and tax planning. In the Owens family situation they did, indeed, avoid the costs of Probate. But the Capital Gains tax consequences were many times the cost of Probate. More frustrating for the Owens, they learned much too late that using a Trust would have saved them from Probate and Capital Gains tax. The deceased owner purchased the property for $200,000 – this was his cost basis. At the time of his death the property had appreciated to $800,000. The Owens children wanted to immediately sell. Doing so resulted in a gain of $600,000. The Owens owed $90,000 in Capital Gains taxes in the tax bracket they were in at the time—the lowest of the Capital Gains tax brackets. Without joint tenancy the property's cost basis would have been stepped-up to $800,000 and no Capital Gain tax would have been due.

The example of the Owens family and the implications of using joint tenancy for real estate inheritance is helpful in understanding the concept of stepped-up basis and how it affects estate planning and capital gains taxes. The stepped-up basis is an adjustment of the cost basis of inherited property to its fair market value at the time of the original owner's death. This adjustment can significantly reduce Capital Gains taxes when the property is sold by the heirs.

For instance, if a home was purchased for $100,000 (the cost basis) and its value at the time of the owner's death is $300,000, avoiding joint tenancy would allow the cost basis to be stepped-up to $300,000. If the heirs later sell the home for $1,000,000, they would be taxed only on the gain above $300,000, rather than the gain above the original purchase price of $100,000. This mechanism can offer a substantial tax advantage, effectively making a significant portion of the Capital Gain tax-free. This is a tax savings, in 2024, of $30,000 to $40,000 depending on the tax bracket of the Seller.

The lack of a stepped-up basis in a joint tenancy arrangement can lead to a significant tax burden, as seen in the Owens family's situation. Without the stepped-up basis, the entire gain from the original purchase price to the sale price could be subject to Capital Gains tax, reducing the inheritance's value and potentially causing financial strain and conflicts within the family.

To navigate these complexities, families like the Owens' should consider estate planning strategies beyond joint tenancy, such as Trusts or other mechanisms that can offer a stepped-up basis and other benefits. For example, a properly structured Trust can ensure that assets are passed on to heirs with a stepped-up basis, minimizing Capital Gains taxes and preserving more of the estate's value for the next generation. Additionally, consulting with estate planning professionals can help families tailor their estate planning to their specific circumstances, potentially avoiding the pitfalls of joint tenancy and similar arrangements.

In another scenario, the Johnson siblings inherited a rental property through joint tenancy from their parents, unaware of the tax consequences that awaited them. As they contemplated selling the property to reinvest in their own ventures, the shock of substantial Capital Gains tax liabilities loomed large. The lack of a stepped-up basis left the siblings owing large Capital Gains taxes. This tax debt forced them to reassess their investment plans. They were counting on using the full value of the property in their new ventures. But, instead, they came up short because they had to pay the Capital Gains tax.

The critical issue at play with the Johnson siblings is the substantial Capital Gains tax liability due to the lack of a stepped-up basis. Again, stepped-up basis is a tax benefit that resets the value of an inherited asset to its market value at the time of the death of the person from whom the real estate was inherited. Without this benefit, the Johnsons face taxes on all gains from the property's original purchase price to its current sale price.

Joint tenancy, while offering simplicity and avoiding Probate, does not provide the stepped-up basis benefit, leading to higher Capital Gains tax if the property has appreciated. Using joint tenancy creates the possibility of other problems in addition to the loss of the step-up in basis. It is possible that the person who is named as a joint tenant, for the purpose of avoiding Probate, actually dies before the original owner. In such a case, joint tenancy provides no benefit, and the real property will require Probate with all the risks Probate entails. It is also possible that the person who is added to title as a joint tenant to avoid Probate has debts, creditors, even judgments. If so, the real estate is subject to the debts of the joint tenant.

Sometimes creative parents add one of their children as a joint tenant to avoid Probate with the understanding that upon the parent's death the child will sell the property and distribute the proceeds equally among all the siblings. This sounds like a win-win solution for everyone but there are two obvious problems. First, of course, is the step-up in basis loss discussed above. The second is that the child whose name is placed on title as a joint tenant is not legally bound to sell the property or distribute the proceeds among the siblings. There is nothing legally to require this to happen.

In light of the risks and challenges posed by joint tenancy in real property succession, it is imperative for individuals to adopt strategic planning strategies to mitigate the financial hurdles and preserve family wealth across generations. By understanding the implications of losing the step-up in basis and facing Capital Gains tax liabilities, families can explore alternative estate planning options. Seeking professional guidance from estate planning experts and tax advisors can provide valuable insights and tailored solutions to navigate the complexities of generational wealth transfer and minimize the impact of taxation on family assets.

The perils of joint tenancy in real property succession extend beyond the practical aspects of ownership. They encompass significant financial risks related to the loss of the step-up in basis, Capital Gains tax liabilities for Beneficiaries, death of the joint tenant, greed of the joint tenant and subjecting the property to the creditors of the joint tenant.

Please note that similar in many ways to joint tenancy, twenty-nine states (at this writing) have adopted a deed known as the "Transfer on Death" deed. "Transfer on Death" deed, also known as a "Beneficiary deed" in some jurisdictions, is a legal document that allows property owners to name one or more Beneficiaries to whom the property will automatically transfer upon the owner's death. This deed operates similarly to a life insurance policy or a payable-on-death bank account, where the asset passes directly to the Beneficiary named in the deed.

Many estate planning lawyers believe the Transfer on Death deed has many more disadvantages than it does advantages. While it promises ease of transfer on death by avoiding Probate, it provides no protection if the named Beneficiary has a disability at the time the transfer takes place. This critical issue is discussed in Chapter Fourteen. It provides no protection against conflict or legal challenge. It does not address debts and taxes owed by the estate, potentially leaving Beneficiaries responsible for settling these obligations without having access to the property to do so. Additionally, the simplicity of changing the Transfer on Death deed's Beneficiary might result in unintended consequences, particularly if the property owner makes changes during times of diminished capacity or under undue influence, raising questions about the deed's validity.

By recognizing the implications of these risks, individuals should make informed decisions, adopt strategic planning measures, and seek expert guidance to safeguard family assets, preserve the family legacy, and secure the value of real property for future generations.

"Planning is bringing the future into the present so that you can do something about it now."

—ALAN LAKEIN

"You must plan for things you think can never happen. Life has a way of blindsiding us with unexpected challenges."

—UNKNOWN

"In preparing for battle I have always found that plans are useless, but planning is indispensable."

—DWIGHT D. EISENHOWER

CHAPTER SIX

The Devastating Impact of Incapacity

In planning for death, one often overlooked yet critical aspect is planning for potential incapacity. The consequences of failing to address this vital issue can be severe, resulting in significant hardships for both the individual and their family. In this Chapter, we will discuss the legal and practical ramifications of becoming incapacitated, exploring the costs, difficulties, and risks associated with Court-appointed Guardians and Conservators. We also shine a light on the transformative benefits of having a properly written Durable Power of Attorney in place.

Imagine a scenario where a beloved family member suddenly becomes incapacitated due to a debilitating illness or unforeseen accident. The once vibrant and independent individual is now unable to make decisions or manage their affairs. In such situations, the family is faced with many challenges, both emotionally and legally.

A Power of Attorney is a legal document you can create to give another the authority to act on your behalf. That person is called the "Attorney in Fact." If you lose the ability to act for yourself, the authority of your Attorney in Fact ends. This is a problem.

Every State in the Nation has enacted laws to enable Attorneys in Fact to continue to act on behalf of the person who appointed them regardless of that person's ability to act on their own. This kind of Power of Attorney is called a "Durable Power of Attorney." As long as the Durable Power of Attorney was written correctly, the Attorney in Fact's authority to act on behalf of the Principal, the person who appointed the Attorney in Fact, will continue regardless of the condition of the Principal. Only death or revocation by the Principal will terminate the Attorney in Fact's authority. A well-crafted Durable Power of Attorney is an essential part of proper legal planning to protect your family—it is critical.

The alternative to a well-written Durable Power of Attorney is the legal process of obtaining a Court-appointed Guardian and Conservator. A Conservator is given authority over a person's financial concerns; a Guardian is given authority over the actual person. While Guardianship and Conservatorship are well defined in the law, both as to authority and the steps to appoint, the actual process is fraught with difficulties, complexities, and challenges. For example, before the Court will appoint one human being to control another, it must be convinced that the Ward (the term for the incapacitated person) is incapacitated. Any hint that the Ward is not incapacitated, and the Court will require extensive evidence. Evidence requires litigation, lawyers, money, etc. And this is only the first of numerous hurdles. Such a process should be avoided if possible.

The Jensen family's world was turned upside down when their father, Adam,

suffered a stroke that left him incapacitated. Without a Durable Power of Attorney in place, the family found themselves entangled in a legal maze. Seeking help and advice from extended family, friends, their Church, and several Social Services Agencies, they eventually discovered that they would need to engage a lawyer and seek a Court-appointed Guardian and Conservator. After many delays and significant expense, a Court-appointed Guardian and Conservator was assigned to make decisions on Adam's behalf.

A routine petition for Guardianship and Conservatorship takes weeks, sometimes months, and several thousand dollars—if uncontested. Adam's matter became quite complex when some in the family did not agree on who should be appointed. Adam's wife was not the mother of Adam's children. Many Court hearings were held, and tens of thousands of dollars spent until finally Adam's wife capitulated and withdrew. No one expected this conflict and high emotions. Legally Adam's wife had the best claim to be appointed. But she did not have the emotional or financial reserves to finish the battle. Sue Jensen, Adam's wife, learned the hard way that failing to plan for incapacity can have devastating legal, financial and emotional consequences.

Clara's story is a reminder of the emotional toll of incapacity. When her mother, Edna Thompson, was diagnosed with dementia, Clara became her primary caregiver. This was difficult enough, but soon she learned that being available and willing to take care of her mother was not enough. Managing her mother's affairs required legal authority. Navigating complex legal processes while witnessing Edna's decline took a toll on Clara's mental and emotional well-being. She was told by the lawyer helping her in obtaining the Order of Guardianship and Conservatorship that if Edna had prepared a Durable Power of Attorney none of the time or money would have been needed to help her mother.

In cases where a Durable Power of Attorney is absent, it takes a Court Order to appoint Guardians and Conservators to make decisions on behalf of the incapacitated individual. While this Court process is well defined in the law, it can often be far from routine. It always takes time and money and is open to expensive challenges. All Courts are hesitant to give one human being authority over another if there is any doubt. Doubt is often not difficult to create.

The Nelson family's experience serves as a cautionary tale of the high costs associated with this Court-Appointed process. When George Johnson became incapacitated following a car accident, his family was shocked by the mounting legal fees and Court costs involved in establishing a Guardianship and Conservatorship. The financial strain of Court involvement jeopardized the family's financial stability. Before the accident, George was an active entrepreneur with several business ventures—some known by his family and some unknown. It seemed each venture discovered had different partners. Each partner thought their venture was the most pressing with the most to gain or lose. Each had their story to tell the Court. The problem was, of course, you do not just write the Judge a letter to tell your story. The process of litigation is complex and ordered. It took years and overwhelming financial resources, especially when considering the amounts spent by all the parties together. George's eldest son Robert was eventually appointed. All of this would have been avoided by a well-written Durable Power of Attorney.

Leanne's story epitomizes the loss of personal choice and privacy that accompanies Court-Appointed Guardianships and Conservatorships. When her uncle, Fred Iverson, fell ill and required a Guardian and Conservator, Leanne witnessed strangers making decisions on his behalf without considering his preferences. The intrusion into Fred's personal affairs not only infringed on his autonomy but also strained family relationships. Leanne was not directly involved in the Court process. From what she could determine after the appointment was made, none of Fred's immediate family were actively involved. They were overwhelmed by the entire legal process and left the details to lawyers and Social Workers. In the end a stranger was appointed. To Leanne it seemed dehumanizing and oppressive to see this happen to her beloved Uncle Fred.

The case of Sofia Ramirez sheds light on the risks of abuse and exploitation in Court- Appointed Guardianships and Conservatorships. Without a designated Attorney in Fact to oversee her affairs, Sofia fell victim to financial exploitation by her Court-Appointed Conservator. The lack of accountability and oversight in the process left Sofia vulnerable to manipulation, harm, and exploitation. Sofia was new to the community with her family living some distance away in another State. The Court appointed a professional Guardian as the Guardian and Conservator. While accountability is part of the legal process, it is not unheard of for the system to be manipulated, which in Sofia's case it was.

Amidst the bleak landscape of incapacity planning, a well-written Durable Power of Attorney stands as a beacon of hope, empowerment and a fortress of protection. This legal document grants the chosen Attorney in Fact the authority to make decisions on behalf of the incapacitated person, following their predetermined instructions and preferences.

The Haroldson family's experience highlights the importance of ensuring continuity of care through a Durable Power of Attorney. When Eva Haroldson's health declined rapidly, her chosen Attorney in Fact, Claudia, was able to make timely decisions in accordance with her mother's wishes. The seamless transition of decision-making preserved Eva's dignity and autonomy.

In the case of the Martinez family, the existence of a well-written Durable Power of Attorney brought peace of mind during a challenging time. When Juan Martinez became incapacitated, his wife, Elena Martinez, was able to manage their finances and make critical decisions with confidence and without the interference of unwanted busybodies. The clarity provided by the Durable Power of Attorney alleviated stress and uncertainty, fostering harmony within the family and ensuring Juan's well-being.

The Cannon family's story exemplifies the proactive approach to incapacity planning through a Durable Power of Attorney. By appointing an Attorney in Fact whom the Cannons trusted to act on their behalf, the Cannons avoided the need for costly litigation in both time and money, not to mention emotion. This foresight preserved their assets and their autonomy. It also saved the family from the oppressive distraction of legal processes when they needed to focus on caring for their loved ones.

The consequences of becoming incapacitated without a proper plan in place are far-reaching and profound. From the financial burdens of litigation to the loss of personal autonomy and privacy—the risks are significant. Embracing the empowering tool of a well-written Durable Power of Attorney will enable you to protect your interests, safeguard your family's well-being and ensure peace of mind during extremely challenging times.

"*You must take action now that will move you towards your goals. Develop a sense of urgency in your life.*"

—H. JACKSON BROWN, JR.

"*Trusts are essential for anyone who wishes to maintain control over how their estate is used and how it is distributed after they're gone.*"

—UNKNOWN

"*Only put off until tomorrow what you are willing to die having left undone.*"

—PICASSO

CHAPTER SEVEN

The Trust

Trusts have long stood as a cornerstone of legal and financial arrangements, evolving from simple medieval safeguards to complex instruments of modern asset management and estate planning. A Trust establishes a fiduciary relationship in which a Trustee holds property or assets for a Beneficiary's benefit. This Chapter explores the historical origins, evolution, and modern applications of Trusts, highlighting their enduring significance and adaptability across centuries.

The concept of the Trust traces back to medieval England, a period marked by the Crusades. Knights leaving for battle entrusted their estates to stewards, laying the groundwork for the Trust as a means to manage and protect assets in the owner's absence. This necessity gave rise to an early form of Trust, ensuring the welfare of the knight's family and the continuity of estate management.

The formal recognition of Trusts in English common law was pivotal to their development. Trusts provided a flexible solution to the rigidity of feudal property laws, enabling landowners to secure the future of their estates beyond the constraints of inheritance laws and feudal obligations. This period saw the crystallization of Trusts as legal entities capable of holding and managing property independent of the landowner's personal circumstances.

The Protestant Reformation and subsequent legal reforms, such as the Statute of Charitable Uses of 1601, expanded the scope of Trusts. Charitable Trusts emerged as tools for social welfare, supporting education, poverty relief, and other public goods. This era underscored the potential of Trusts to serve not only individual family interests but also broader societal needs.

The 19th century's industrial boom brought about significant wealth expansion, propelling Trusts into the realm of business and industry. Corporate Trusts controlled major industry sectors, demonstrating the Trust's capacity for economic influence. However, the monopolistic power of these Trusts eventually led to public outcry and legal intervention.

In response to the monopolistic practices of Corporate Trusts, the United States enacted the Sherman Antitrust Act of 1890. This landmark legislation aimed to dismantle business monopolies and foster competition, highlighting the need for legal frameworks to regulate the economic power concentrated in Trusts.

In contemporary society, Trusts have become integral to estate planning. They offer strategic advantages in asset management, tax planning and privacy protection. Trusts facilitate the transfer of assets, avoiding the Probate process and ensuring the Grantor's wishes are fulfilled efficiently and discreetly.

The philanthropic tradition of Trusts continues with Charitable Trusts playing a pivotal role in funding education, healthcare and various social initiatives. These Trusts exemplify the enduring capacity of Trusts to channel resources towards public welfare.

The development of Special Needs Trusts marks a significant evolution in Trust law, addressing the nuanced needs of Beneficiaries with disabilities. These Trusts ensure that individuals can receive financial support without compromising their eligibility for government benefits, reflecting a sophisticated approach to Beneficiary care.

The business world has seen innovative uses of Trusts, such as Real Estate Investment Trusts (REITs), which have democratized access to real estate investments. REITs allow individuals to invest in property portfolios, showcasing the Trust's adaptability to new investment models.

The journey of Trusts from medieval estate management tools to sophisticated instruments of modern financial and legal practice underscores their versatility and resilience. Trusts have adapted to meet the evolving needs of society, balancing individual interests with broader societal goals. As legal and financial landscapes continue to evolve, the Trust remains a testament to the enduring importance of flexible, secure mechanisms for asset management and philanthropy. Through centuries of innovation, Trusts have proven themselves as indispensable components of the legal and financial fabric, poised to meet future challenges and opportunities.

In the realm of estate planning, preparing for the future management and distribution of one's assets is a paramount concern. Among the various strategies at one's disposal, the creation of a Trust stands out as a particularly effective tool. Designed to bridge the present with the future, Trusts offer a sophisticated means of ensuring that your assets are managed and distributed according to your wishes, with a level of control and flexibility that other estate planning tools do not provide.

Imagine a family gathered in a lawyer's office, anxious and uncertain about their future following the patriarch's passing. This scenario, all too common, lays the groundwork for our exploration into Trusts, a cornerstone of estate planning that offers both solace and structure in such times. Through the lens of this family's journey, we will unravel the elements of Trusts, transforming abstract legal principles into tangible life lessons.

What is a Trust?

At its core, a Trust is a contract, it is a legal arrangement characterized by a three-party relationship. It involves the transfer of property or assets from the owner (the Trustor, sometimes referred to as the Settlor, always referred to by the IRS as the Grantor) to a trusted individual or institution (the Trustee), who then manages these assets for the benefit of others (the Beneficiaries). Trusts are versatile instruments, capable of serving various purposes—from safeguarding assets for future generations, to providing for charitable endeavors, to offering a structured means of asset distribution that aligns with the Grantor's intentions.

Let's consider a patriarch John who, aware of life's unpredictability, decided to establish a Trust. John's story is not unique but his foresight in using a Trust to manage his family's future is a testament to the power of thoughtful planning. A Trust, in essence, allowed John to appoint his trusted sister Elizabeth as the Trustee, charging her with the responsibility of managing his assets for his children's benefit after his passing. This legal arrangement, rooted in centuries of common law and detailed in statutes like the Uniform Trust Code, illustrates the Trust's role as a bridge between generations, safeguarding a family's financial security.

Parties to a Trust

1. The Grantor (or Settlor): This is the individual who creates the Trust, transferring ownership of

their assets into the Trust's care.

2. The Trustee: Tasked with the Trust's administration, the Trustee manages the Trust's assets responsibly and in accordance with the Trust's terms for the benefit of the Beneficiaries.

3. The Beneficiary: Beneficiaries are those who receive the benefits from the Trust, which could be in the form of financial support, income, or other assets as dictated by the Trust's terms.

John the Grantor, Elizabeth the Trustee, and John's children, the Beneficiaries, embody the Trust's three-party structure. Each role is crucial: John's vision, Elizabeth's stewardship, and the children's future well-being. This illustration highlights the legal requirements for each party—John's intention, Elizabeth's fiduciary duties, and the children's rights to benefit from the Trust. Their story, hopefully, brings to life the legal definitions and duties outlined in Trust law, making the abstract principles tangible and understandable.

How a Trust is Created

Creating a Trust typically involves the drafting of a Trust document which outlines the Trust's terms, the duties of the Trustee, and the rights of the Beneficiaries. Essential elements for creating a Trust include a clear intention by the Grantor to establish the Trust, a defined purpose, identifiable property or assets to fund the Trust, and the appointment of a Trustee. Trusts can be established during the Grantor's lifetime (living Trusts) or upon their death through a Will (testamentary Trusts).

John's journey to creating a Trust began with a simple desire to ensure his children's welfare without burdening them with immediate financial management responsibilities. By drafting a Trust document with legal assistance, John detailed his wishes, from the distribution of assets to the care of his minor children. This process, governed by legal statutes, showcases the practical steps required to translate personal wishes into a legally binding agreement, ensuring John's legacy is preserved exactly as he envisioned.

Administration of a Trust

The administration of a Trust involves the Trustee managing the Trust's assets according to its terms. This includes investing the Trust's assets prudently, making distributions to Beneficiaries as stipulated, and performing all duties with the Beneficiaries' interests in mind. Trustees are also responsible for paying taxes on behalf of the Trust and maintaining accurate records of the Trust's activities.

Elizabeth's role as Trustee is far from ceremonial. She must navigate the complexities of asset management, from investing the Trust's funds prudently to making distributions to John's children according to the Trust's terms. Her journey is a vivid illustration of the Trustee's responsibilities, underscored by legal principles that demand loyalty, prudence, and impartiality. Elizabeth's story, fraught with challenges and triumphs, underscores the significance of the Trustee's role in fulfilling the Grantor's vision.

Trusts as a Will Substitute

Trusts often serve as an effective substitute for Wills. One of the primary advantages of a Trust is its ability to bypass the Probate process, a legal proceeding that is time-consuming and costly. Unlike Wills, which become public record through Probate, Trusts maintain privacy concerning the details of asset distribution. Additionally, Trusts offer a higher degree of control over when and how Beneficiaries receive assets, allowing for more nuanced estate planning.

John's decision to use a Trust instead of a traditional Will was driven by a desire to protect his family's privacy and bypass the time-consuming and public Probate process. This choice is shared by many, reflecting a common legal strategy to ensure a smooth, private transfer of assets. Through John's foresight, his family experienced a seamless transition, avoiding the Probate Court's delays and public scrutiny—a real-world application of the legal benefits Trusts offer.

Avoiding Probate

The ability of Trusts to avoid Probate is among their most valued features. Since the Trust, rather than the deceased's estate, holds the assets, these assets are not subject to the Probate process. This direct transfer mechanism ensures a more efficient and private distribution of assets to Beneficiaries, free from the potential delays and public scrutiny associated with Probate.

The story of John's Trust serves as a case study in avoiding Probate. With the assets titled in the Trust's name, they pass directly to John's children under Elizabeth's stewardship, sidestepping the Probate system entirely. This strategic planning exemplifies how legal principles translate into practical benefits, offering a quicker, more private means of asset distribution that Probate cannot match.

Through the example of John's family, we see the tangible impact of legal principles from the creation and administration of Trusts to their role in avoiding Probate and acting as a Will substitute. John's story is but one of many, each reflecting the unique potential of Trusts to secure a legacy and provide for future generations with foresight, care and precision.

Trusts represent a cornerstone of comprehensive estate planning, offering a blend of flexibility, control and efficiency that is hard to match. By providing a structured way to manage and distribute assets, Trusts can fulfill a wide range of personal and financial objectives, from ensuring the welfare of loved ones to supporting philanthropic causes. While the intricacies of Trust creation and administration suggest the need for professional guidance, the benefits of incorporating a Trust into one's estate plan are clear. With their ability to bypass Probate, preserve privacy and offer tailored solutions for asset distribution, Trusts are an invaluable tool for anyone looking to secure their legacy and provide for future generations.

As illustrated, Trusts are sophisticated legal mechanisms that serve a myriad of purposes, ranging from estate planning and asset protection to charitable giving and tax efficiency. Each type of Trust comes with its own set of rules, advantages and limitations, making it crucial to understand their distinct characteristics. Below is a brief overview of some of the different kinds of Trusts used today, their strengths, weaknesses, benefits, drawbacks and the reasons for their utilization.

Revocable Trusts (Living Trusts)

Revocable Trusts are also known as Living Trusts because they are created by the Grantor during the Grantor's life. The IRS refers to them as "Grantor" Trusts. They are characterized by their flexibility. The Grantor, Settlor or Trustor retains the power to modify or revoke the Trust at any point during their lifetime. This adaptability is particularly beneficial for managing changes in family dynamics, financial situations or estate planning goals.

Extended Benefits: Beyond avoiding Probate, Revocable Trusts can provide seamless management of assets in the event of the Grantor's incapacity, preventing the need for a Court-appointed Conservatorship. This ensures that the Grantor's financial affairs remain private and are managed according to their wishes, even if they are no longer able to make decisions themselves.

Notable Weaknesses: Despite their benefits, Revocable Trusts do not offer protection against creditors during the Grantor's lifetime. Assets within the Trust are still considered part of the Grantor's taxable estate, which may not be advantageous for those with estate tax concerns or with creditor concerns.

Irrevocable Trusts

The irrevocable nature of these Trusts means that once established, the Grantor relinquishes control over the assets and cannot unilaterally modify the Trust's terms. This loss of control is a legal strategy to remove the assets from the Grantor's estate, thus offering potential savings on estate taxes and protection from creditors.

Extended Benefits: Irrevocable Trusts can be structured in numerous ways to achieve specific goals, such as Life Insurance Trusts designed to exclude life insurance proceeds from the taxable estate or Grantor Retained Annuity Trusts (GRATs) that allow the Settlor to transfer asset growth out of their estate.

Notable Weaknesses: The permanent decision to transfer assets can be daunting and the irrevocable nature may not suit most people's needs, especially if financial circumstances or relationships change. The Capital Gains advantage of the step-up in basis can be lost using an Irrevocable Trust.

Charitable Trusts

Charitable Trusts embody philanthropic intent while providing financial benefits to the Grantor. Charitable Lead Trusts (CLTs) and Charitable Remainder Trusts (CRTs) are two primary types, each offering a different approach to charitable giving and personal financial benefits.

Extended Benefits: These Trusts can significantly reduce estate and gift taxes by removing assets from the estate while fulfilling philanthropic goals. They also offer the Grantor income tax deductions and can be structured to provide an income stream.

Notable Weaknesses: The irrevocability of Charitable Trusts and the requirement to commit a portion of assets to charity may not align with everyone's estate planning objectives; especially, if personal financial circumstances change.

Special Needs Trusts

Tailored to support individuals with disabilities, Special Needs Trusts, also referred to as Supplemental Needs Trusts, ensure Beneficiaries maintain eligibility for vital government benefits. These Trusts fund supplementary needs beyond what government assistance covers, enhancing the Beneficiary's quality of life without jeopardizing their benefits.

Extended Benefits: The Trust can cover a wide range of expenses, including personal care attendants, out-of-pocket medical costs, and educational expenses, providing flexibility and support that government programs do not offer.

Notable Weaknesses: The Trust must be carefully structured to avoid disqualifying the Beneficiary from government assistance, requiring specialized legal expertise to navigate the complex rules surrounding these benefits.

Spendthrift Trusts

Designed to protect Beneficiaries from their own potential financial irresponsibility or external creditors, Spendthrift Trusts restrict direct access to the Trust assets, ensuring the assets are managed wisely and according to the Grantor's wishes.

Extended Benefits: These Trusts are particularly useful in protecting the inheritance from Beneficiaries' creditors, including future divorce settlements or bankruptcy claims, thereby preserving the assets for the intended purposes.

Notable Weaknesses: The restrictions imposed can sometimes be too limiting for Beneficiaries who may need access to the assets for legitimate reasons, potentially causing tension and challenges within families.

Trusts are a cornerstone of sophisticated estate planning, offering nuanced solutions tailored to individual needs and objectives. Whether aiming to minimize taxes, protect assets, provide for loved ones or support charitable causes, there is a Trust structure available to meet those goals. However, the complexity and permanent nature of some Trusts necessitate careful consideration and expert guidance. By understanding the unique attributes and implications of each Trust type, individuals can make informed decisions that align with their values and estate planning objectives, ensuring their legacy is preserved and their Beneficiaries are cared for according to their wishes.

"A man that does not plan long ahead will find trouble at his door."
—CONFUCIUS

"I'd rather interview 50 people and not hire anyone than hire the wrong person."
—JEFF BEZOS

"Perhaps the most important decision…is the selection of the person to oversee your financial affairs if you are unable to do so."
—JOHN M. GORALKA

CHAPTER EIGHT

Choosing Your Successor Trustee

The Grantor of the Trust, or the person who sets up the Trust, is almost always the initial Trustee. Upon the death or incapacity of the Grantor, a Successor Trustee under the terms of the Trust becomes the Trustee. Choosing who will succeed you as Trustee may be the most important decision you will make in relation to the Trust Centered Estate Plan.

Among the many things to consider in choosing the Successor Trustee are two characteristics that are by far more important than all other considerations. The Successor Trustee must be honest, and the Successor Trustee must be responsible and able to get things done. Other considerations may be important, but they are much less important than these two.

It is important to keep this in mind as you read this Chapter. This Chapter will go into some detail on many aspects of Trust Administration and choosing a Successor Trustee. But as you read, keep these two characteristics foremost in your mind.

Let's look closely at the intricate world of Trust Administration, a domain where legal precision meets personal commitment and where the responsibilities of today shape the legacies of tomorrow. This Chapter will serve as a comprehensive guide for both Grantors, and Successor Trustees, the individuals or entities charged with carrying out the Trust's directives after the Grantor's incapacitation or death.

Trusts are powerful tools for estate planning, offering a means to manage and protect assets, provide for loved ones and ensure that a Grantor's wishes are honored across time. However, the effectiveness of a Trust hinges on the careful planning of the Grantor and the diligence, integrity and skill of the Trustee in administration. This Chapter aims to bridge the gap between the theoretical underpinnings of Trust Law and the practical realities of Trust Administration, providing a solid foundation for both novice and experienced Trustees to succeed in their roles.

For the Grantor: Laying the Groundwork

The initial subsections of this Chapter are dedicated to Grantors, guiding them through the critical process of establishing a Trust, selecting a Successor Trustee and communicating their vision and expectations clearly. These sections underscore the importance of thoughtful preparation and selection, ensuring that the chosen Trustee is not only capable and reliable but also aligned with the Grantor's values and objectives.

For the Successor Trustee: Navigating Responsibilities

The heart of this Chapter investigates the multifaceted responsibilities of the Successor Trustee from understanding the Trust document and managing assets to communicating with Beneficiaries and navigating legal requirements. These sections provide a roadmap for effective Trust Administration. Highlighted are the common pitfalls to avoid, the importance of professional guidance and strategies for managing both the financial and interpersonal aspects of the role.

Bridging Expectations: A Collaborative Approach

A central theme of this guide is the collaborative nature of Trust Administration. It emphasizes the importance of open communication and cooperation between the Grantor, the Trustee and the Beneficiaries. This collaborative approach not only facilitates the smooth operation of the Trust but also helps to preserve family harmony and ensure that the Trust achieves its intended purposes.

As we step into the exploration of Trust Administration, this Chapter serves as both a map and a compass for Grantors and Trustees alike. Whether you are drafting a Trust for the first time, stepping into the role of a Successor Trustee or seeking to deepen your understanding of Trust Administration, this discussion is designed to equip you with the knowledge, skills and confidence needed to navigate the challenges and opportunities that lie ahead.

In the realm of Trust Administration, knowledge is more than power—it is the key to fulfillment, integrity and the successful stewardship of one's legacy. Let's begin this journey together with the aim of mastering the art and science of Trust administration.

The Role and Responsibilities of a Successor Trustee

In the landscape of Estate Planning and Trust management, understanding the role of a Successor Trustee is paramount for both the creators of Trusts and the Beneficiaries. A Successor Trustee is a person or institution appointed to manage the Trust's assets once the original Trustee is unable to do so due to incapacity, resignation or death. This section looks into the definition of a Successor Trustee, exploring their legal and ethical duties to manage the Trust's assets in accordance with the Trust document and for the ultimate benefit of the Beneficiaries.

A Successor Trustee stands as the linchpin in the

effective management and execution of a Trust after the original Trustee can no longer fulfill their duties. Unlike the original Trustee, who may also be the Grantor, the Successor Trustee is often a third party—either an individual or a financial institution. This designation is crucial for ensuring the continuity of Trust management without the need for Court intervention, which can be devastatingly time-consuming and costly.

Legal and Ethical Duties

The Successor Trustee's primary responsibilities are governed by both the Trust document and State law, which collectively outline their legal and ethical obligations. These duties are manifold and require the Successor Trustee to act with the utmost fidelity and prudence. Key responsibilities include:

1. Adherence to the Trust Document: The Successor Trustee must thoroughly understand the Trust document because it is the blueprint that guides all Trust-related decisions. This includes following the specific instructions laid out by the Grantor regarding asset distribution, Beneficiary support and any other directives.

2. Asset Management: The Successor Trustee is charged with the prudent management of the Trust's assets. This encompasses a range of activities from investing the Trust's assets wisely to ensure their growth, to protecting them from undue

risk and loss. The Successor Trustee must balance the need for asset preservation with the desire to generate income for the Beneficiaries, as outlined in the Trust document.

3. Beneficiary Communication: Maintaining open and transparent communication with the Trust's Beneficiaries is critical. The Successor Trustee may be required under the terms of the Trust to provide Beneficiaries with regular updates regarding the Trust's assets, its administration and any distributions made.

4. Fiduciary Duty: Above all, the Successor Trustee has a fiduciary duty to act in the best interest of the Beneficiaries. This means managing the Trust's assets with loyalty, care and impartiality, ensuring that no Beneficiary is favored over another unless the Trust document explicitly dictates such preference. Fiduciary duties require the Trustee to put the interests of the Beneficiary above their own interests.

5. Tax and Legal Compliance: The Successor Trustee is also responsible for ensuring that the Trust complies with all relevant tax laws and regulations. This includes filing any required tax returns and paying any taxes owed by the Trust in a timely manner.

6. Distribution of Assets: Finally, the Successor Trustee is tasked with distributing the Trust's assets to the Beneficiaries in accordance with the terms of the Trust document. This process must be executed

in a timely way and with care to ensure that each Beneficiary receives their due share as specified by the Grantor.

The role of a Successor Trustee is both a privilege and a profound responsibility. It requires an individual or institution that is not only trustworthy and reliable but also responsible in navigating the complex interplay of legal, financial and ethical considerations inherent in managing a Trust. By fulfilling their duties with diligence and integrity, the Successor Trustee ensures that the Grantor's wishes are honored and that the Beneficiaries' interests are safeguarded, thereby upholding the Trust's purpose and legacy.

The Evolution of Trustee Roles: Initial Trustee to Successor Trustee

The dynamics of a Trust change notably with the transition from an initial Trustee to a Successor Trustee. This evolution is not merely a change of hands but a shift in perspective, responsibilities and sometimes the authority underpinning the Trust's administration. Understanding these differences is crucial for both the drafting of Trust documents and the seamless execution of the Trust's purpose.

The initial Trustee serves as both its architect and guardian. This dual role embodies the vision for the Trust, the selection of Beneficiaries and the initial management and protection of its assets. The initial

Trustee's responsibilities are foundational, setting the stage for the Trust's objectives and how they are to be achieved. These responsibilities include:

1. Defining the Trust's Terms: Articulating the purpose, terms, and conditions under which the Trust operates, including Beneficiary designations and distribution plans.

2. Funding the Trust: Transferring assets into the Trust to fund its operations and benefit its intended recipients.

3. Asset Management: Making strategic decisions about how the Trust's assets are invested and managed, balancing growth with risk to meet the Trust's long-term objectives.

4. Beneficiary Communication: Establishing the precedent for if, how and when Beneficiaries are informed about the Trust's status, distributions and any other relevant information.

The role of the Successor Trustee, activated upon the incapacity, resignation or death of the Initial Trustee, is marked by a shift from establishment and strategic positioning to stewardship and execution. The Successor Trustee inherits a framework and set of objectives already in motion, with the primary task of following the roadmap laid out by the Grantor while adapting to any unforeseen circumstances or changes in the Trust's environment. Key aspects of this transition include:

1. Adhering to Established Terms: The Successor

Trustee's actions are guided by the Trust document created by the Grantor, requiring an understanding of its terms and a commitment to executing its instructions faithfully.

2. Continuity and Adaptation: While maintaining the Trust's strategic direction, the Successor Trustee must also adapt to changes in the economic landscape, Beneficiary needs and legal requirements, ensuring the Trust remains effective and compliant.

3. Active Asset Management: The responsibility for managing the Trust's assets continues, with a focus on preserving and growing the estate within the risk parameters set forth by the Trust document.

4. Communication: The Successor Trustee may maintain or establish communication channels with Beneficiaries, providing updates, handling inquiries and managing expectations in line with the document's guidelines.

5. Fiduciary Duty and Impartiality: The Successor Trustee's role is underscored by a fiduciary duty to act in the best interest of the Beneficiaries, always subordinating the Trustee's interest to that of the Beneficiaries. This includes managing the Trust assets with care, skill, prudence and impartiality. Unlike the Initial Trustee, who may have personal connections or intentions for the Trust, the Successor Trustee often must

navigate these relationships with a more detached perspective, focusing solely on the Trust's terms and the Beneficiaries' welfare.

6. Executing Distributions: The Successor Trustee is responsible for executing the distribution plan laid out by the Grantor, which may involve complex decisions about timing, amounts and methods of distribution to ensure fairness and compliance with the Trust's objectives.

7. Legal and Tax Compliance: As laws and tax regulations evolve, the Successor Trustee must ensure that the Trust remains compliant, adapting to new legal requirements and managing tax obligations to minimize liabilities and preserve the Trust's assets.

The transition from an Initial Trustee to a Successor Trustee represents a critical phase in the life cycle of a Trust. It involves not only a change in administration but also a reaffirmation of the Trust's purpose and a commitment to its continuity. By understanding the nuances of these roles and preparing accordingly, both Trustees can ensure that the Trust fulfills its mission, honoring the Grantor's intentions and serving the best interests of the Beneficiaries.

Selecting a Successor Trustee: Essential Qualities and Competencies

Choosing a Successor Trustee is a decision of

paramount importance in the process of Trust planning and management. The individual or institution selected for this role will be responsible for carrying out the Grantor's wishes, managing and protecting the Trust's assets and ensuring the Beneficiaries' interests are served. This Section outlines the key characteristics and competencies that make someone a good candidate for being a Successor Trustee, emphasizing the central qualities of honesty, effectiveness, financial acumen, impartiality and reliability.

At the core of a successful Trustee-Beneficiary relationship is trust, predicated on the honesty of the Trustee. A Successor Trustee must be someone who demonstrates integrity in all aspects of their life, as they will be tasked with making decisions that could significantly impact the financial future of the Beneficiaries. Honesty and communication is essential for maintaining a positive and constructive relationship with the Beneficiaries.

The role of a Successor Trustee involves a broad range of tasks, from administrative duties to financial management and legal compliance. The ability to effectively execute these tasks, often simultaneously and under pressure, is crucial. A good Successor Trustee is not just a planner but an executor who can take decisive action, manage time efficiently and follow through on commitments to ensure the Trust operates smoothly and meets its objectives.

A solid understanding of financial matters, including investment strategies, tax planning, and estate law, is helpful for a Successor Trustee. While not every Trustee needs to be a financial expert, they should have a grasp of financial principles or be willing to consult with experts when necessary. This knowledge enables the Trustee to make informed decisions about asset management, ensuring the Trust's financial health and growth potential are maximized.

Impartiality: Fairness in Decision-Making

A Successor Trustee often faces the delicate task of balancing the interests of multiple Beneficiaries, who may have differing needs and expectations. The ability to remain impartial, making decisions based solely on the Trust's terms and the best interests of all Beneficiaries, is critical. This includes avoiding conflicts of interest and ensuring that personal relationships do not influence the Trustee's actions or decisions.

The Beneficiaries' well-being and the Trust's integrity rely on the Trustee's reliability. This encompasses both the consistency of their actions and their availability when needed. A reliable Successor Trustee is responsive to Beneficiaries' inquiries, provides regular updates on the Trust's status and adheres strictly to the Trust's guidelines and timelines for distributions and other key events.

Effective communication is a pivotal skill for a Successor Trustee. They must be able to convey complex information in a clear, understandable manner to Beneficiaries, who may not have a background in financial or legal matters. Additionally, the Trustee should possess strong negotiation and conflict-resolution skills to navigate any disputes that arise among Beneficiaries or external parties.

Selecting a Successor Trustee is a decision that should not be taken lightly. The ideal candidate will embody a combination of honesty, effectiveness, financial acumen, impartiality, reliability and strong communication skills. These qualities ensure that the Trustee can manage the Trust's assets wisely, fulfill the Grantor's intentions and maintain a positive relationship with the Beneficiaries. By prioritizing these characteristics in the selection process, Grantors can provide their Trusts—and their Beneficiaries—with a solid foundation for success.

Navigating the Waters: Family Dynamics and the Successor Trustee Selection

The selection of a Successor Trustee within the context of family dynamics is akin to navigating a complex network of waterways, where the currents of relationships, histories and personal interests converge. This Section examines how family dynamics should influence the choice of a Successor Trustee, exploring the potential for conflicts of interest and strategies for mitigating them to ensure the Trust's successful administration and the harmony among Beneficiaries.

The first step in considering a Successor Trustee

is to map the family landscape, understanding the relationships, alliances and potential fault lines that exist. Family dynamics are rarely straightforward; they are shaped by years of shared history, which can include both positive bonds and unresolved conflicts. Recognizing these dynamics is crucial in anticipating how the selection of a Successor Trustee might impact the family's harmony and the Trust's execution.

Conflicts of interest can arise when a potential Successor Trustee stands to benefit personally from decisions made in the management of the Trust, potentially at the expense of other Beneficiaries. In families, these conflicts can be particularly complex, intertwining financial interests with emotional ties and historical grievances. For example, selecting a family member who is also a Beneficiary could lead to perceptions of bias or favoritism, even if none exist. It's essential to identify these potential conflicts upfront and consider how they might influence the Trust's administration and the family's well-being.

1. Communication: Grantors often believe that open discussions about the selection process, the rationale behind it and how conflicts of interest are being addressed can alleviate concerns and foster trust among family members. Such a rationale seems wise but is often the absolute wrong thing to do. Such conversation can reopen old wounds or create problems where none existed. Extreme care

should always be exercised when discussing "why" you as Grantor choose to do anything. "Why" can always be countered with contrary reasoning by others and can lead to bigger problems than the ones you intended to solve. Be wise. Explaining why may be very foolish. Keep your reasons to yourself.

2. Neutral Third-Party Involvement: In some cases, appointing an independent third party as the Successor Trustee—such as a family friend, attorney or financial advisor—can sidestep potential conflicts, ensuring an impartial administration of the Trust. Professional Trustees are very expensive and often the wrong choice unless there is no viable alternative.

3. Clear Guidelines and Oversight: Establishing clear guidelines for the Successor Trustee's decision-making and setting up mechanisms for oversight can help mitigate potential conflicts. This might include regular audits or reports to Beneficiaries. Of course there exists a competing approach to audits and reports. Some believe that if the Successor Trustee is carefully chosen and fully empowered such audits may not be necessary. The requirement of audits and reports sometimes allows disgruntled persons to use the requirement to force conflict, even litigation.

4. Co-Trustees: While the concept of appointing Co-

Trustees might appear as a balanced approach to mitigate potential biases and ensure fair decision-making, it often introduces its own set of challenges that can paradoxically exacerbate family tensions rather than alleviate them. Co-Trusteeship by its very nature requires a unanimity or a majority in decision-making that can be difficult to achieve, particularly in families with underlying dynamics of discord or differing views on asset management and Beneficiary care. This structure can lead to stalemates where crucial decisions are delayed or worse, lead to outright conflict, as Co-Trustees find themselves entrenched in their positions. Consequently, the wisdom of selecting a single, well-chosen Trustee—and a Successor, should the initial choice be unable to serve—becomes evident. This approach streamlines decision-making, reduces the potential for conflict, and ensures that the Trust's administration remains efficient and effective. It emphasizes the importance of careful Trustee selection, where the chosen individual's integrity, impartiality and capability align with the Trust's objectives and the Beneficiaries' best interests, thereby safeguarding the Trust's smooth operation and the family's harmony.

Beyond the technical skills required for managing a Trust, a Successor Trustee's emotional intelligence can be a critical factor in navigating family dynamics. The ability to understand and manage one's own emotions and to recognize and influence the emotions of others can be invaluable in addressing sensitivities, managing conflicts, and maintaining family harmony.

The selection of a Successor Trustee in the context of family dynamics requires a careful balancing act, considering both the technical competencies needed to manage the Trust and the emotional and relational landscapes of the family. By anticipating potential conflicts of interest and employing strategies to mitigate them, families can navigate these waters successfully, ensuring the Trust fulfills its intended purpose while maintaining family harmony.

The Legal and Financial Duties of a Successor Trustee

The role of a Successor Trustee encompasses a broad spectrum of legal and financial responsibilities essential for the proper administration of a Trust. This pivotal position demands an understanding of the Trust's objectives, as well as a grasp of the legal and financial tasks required to fulfill those objectives. This section outlines the specific legal and financial duties that a Successor Trustee must perform, including managing assets, settling debts, and ensuring compliance with tax laws.

The cornerstone of a Successor Trustee's responsibilities is the prudent management of the Trust's assets. This involves:

1. Inventorying Assets: Taking stock of all the Trust's

assets is the first step, requiring the Successor Trustee to accurately identify and value each asset.

2. Investment Oversight: The Trustee must manage the Trust's investments with a keen eye toward balancing growth with risk, ensuring the investments align with the Trust's objectives and the Beneficiaries' best interests. A wise Trustee will seek experienced and skilled advice from professionals.

3. Asset Protection: Protecting the Trust's assets from loss, whether through insurance, diversification, or other means, is crucial.

A Successor Trustee is responsible for identifying and settling any debts owed by the Trust, as well as, managing ongoing expenses related to the Trust's administration. This includes:

1. Validating Debts: All claims against the Trust must be verified to ensure their legitimacy before payment.

2. Prioritizing and Paying Debts: Some debts may have legal precedence over others, requiring careful management to ensure all obligations are met in the correct order. Sometimes a debt is not a legal debt and is not actually owed. When in doubt, seek legal advice.

3. Managing Operational Expenses: Regular expenses, such as property maintenance, insurance premiums and professional fees need to be managed efficiently

to preserve the Trust's assets.

Tax obligations form a significant part of a Successor Trustee's responsibilities, demanding diligence to ensure the Trust remains in good standing with tax authorities. This involves:

1. Filing Tax Returns: The Trustee must file annual tax returns for the Trust, reporting any income generated by the Trust's assets. This task requires an understanding of the Trust's tax obligations and may necessitate the assistance of a tax professional to navigate the complexities of Trust taxation.

2. Paying Taxes: Beyond filing, the Successor Trustee is responsible for ensuring that any taxes owed by the Trust are paid on time. This includes income taxes, estate taxes (if applicable), and any other taxes that the Trust incurs through its operations or asset management.

3. Tax Planning: Proactive tax planning is crucial to minimize the Trust's tax liabilities. This may involve strategic decisions about distributions, investments and the timing of certain transactions to take advantage of tax efficiencies and exemptions. This should be undertaken with professional advice.

A key financial responsibility of the Successor Trustee is managing distributions to Beneficiaries in accordance with the terms of the Trust document. This requires:

1. Understanding Distribution Terms: The Trustee

must be familiar with the Trust document to ensure distributions are made according to the Grantor's wishes.

2. Timing and Amount of Distributions: Decisions about when and how much to distribute to Beneficiaries often require balancing the Trust's financial health with the Beneficiaries' needs and expectations.

3. Tax Considerations of Distributions: The Trustee may also consider the tax implications of distributions, both for the Trust and the Beneficiaries, making informed decisions to optimize tax outcomes.

Comprehensive record-keeping and regular reporting to Beneficiaries and relevant legal entities are vital to the efficient operation of the Trust. This includes:

1. Maintaining Financial Records: Detailed records of all transactions, including asset management activities, distributions, and expenses, must be kept to provide a clear financial picture of the Trust's operations.

2. Providing Regular Updates: Depending on the terms of the Trust, Beneficiaries should be kept informed about the Trust's financial status, including any significant decisions made by the Trustee regarding asset management or distributions.

3. Preparing Financial Statements: Depending on the terms of the Trust, annual financial statements

that summarize the Trust's financial activities and status may be prepared and made available to Beneficiaries and, if required, to regulatory bodies.

Lastly, the Successor Trustee must ensure that the Trust's administration complies with all relevant laws and regulations. This encompasses:

1. Staying Informed about Legal Changes: Laws governing Trusts can change, necessitating that the Trustee stay informed about any developments that could impact the Trust's administration.

2. Legal Filings and Documentation: Depending on the jurisdiction, there may be legal filings or documentation required to maintain the Trust's legal standing or to document significant actions taken by the Trustee.

3. Protecting Beneficiary Rights: The Trustee must also ensure that the Beneficiaries' rights are protected, adhering to both the letter and the spirit of the Trust document and applicable law.

The legal and financial responsibilities of a Successor Trustee are both extensive and multifaceted, requiring a blend of diligence, expertise and integrity. By fulfilling these duties conscientiously, the Successor Trustee ensures that the Trust operates smoothly, complies with legal requirements, meets its financial obligations and, ultimately, honors the intentions of the Grantor while serving the best interests of the Beneficiaries.

Bridging Expectations: The Successor Trustee's Guide to Managing Beneficiary Relations

The role of a Successor Trustee goes beyond the meticulous management of Trust assets and legal compliance; it encompasses the delicate task of managing Beneficiary expectations and resolving conflicts. This Section provides a guide for Successor Trustees on effective communication strategies, addressing Beneficiary concerns and navigating disputes, ensuring a smooth administration of the Trust and maintaining harmony among its Beneficiaries.

Before discussing the strategies for managing expectations and conflicts, it is crucial for the Successor Trustee to understand the diverse perspectives and expectations of the Beneficiaries. These expectations can vary widely, influenced by individual needs, personal relationships with the Grantor and their understanding (or misunderstanding) of the Trust's terms and purposes. Recognizing these expectations early in the administration process sets the stage for effective communication and conflict resolution.

1. Initial Meeting: Soon after assuming the role, organize an initial meeting with the Beneficiaries to introduce yourself, outline your role, and discuss the Trust's terms and the Beneficiaries' expectations. This meeting can be a cornerstone for building confidence.

2. Regular Updates: Provide regular updates on the Trust's

status, including financial performance, distributions made and any significant decisions regarding the Trust's administration. Consistent communication can preempt misunderstandings and grievances.

3. Accessible Contact: Ensure Beneficiaries know how to reach you and encourage them to communicate their concerns or questions. Being accessible helps in building rapport and confidence with the Beneficiaries.

4. Active Listening: When Beneficiaries express concerns, listen actively and empathetically. Understanding the root of their concerns is the first step in addressing them effectively. When Beneficiaries feel heard they are less inclined to cause the Trustee problems.

5. Educating Beneficiaries: Often, Beneficiary concerns stem from a lack of understanding of Trust principles or the specific terms of the Trust. Providing clear, jargon-free explanations can help alleviate concerns and set realistic expectations.

6. Decision-Making: When making decisions, especially those that may be unpopular, explain your decisions clearly, referencing the Trust document and legal obligations as necessary. Understanding the basis behind decisions can help Beneficiaries accept them even if they disagree.

7. Flexible Approach: Be open to feedback and willing to adjust your approach if it can resolve a conflict

without compromising the Trust's integrity or your fiduciary duties.

8. Legal Guidance: When disputes cannot be resolved through communication, seek legal advice early to ensure that any actions taken are in line with your fiduciary responsibilities and the Trust's terms. When in doubt about anything, seek legal advice from experienced and well-trained lawyers. Any resources spent on seeking professional advice will come from Trust assets. Please, always remember the advice: "an ounce of prevention is worth a pound of cure." Be wise— always seek capable advice timely.

Managing Beneficiary expectations and conflicts requires a blend of communication skills, empathy and a firm understanding of the Trust's terms and legal responsibilities. By establishing open lines of communication, addressing concerns proactively, educating Beneficiaries and employing conflict resolution strategies, when necessary, a Successor Trustee can navigate the complexities of Beneficiary relations. This not only ensures the smooth administration of the Trust but also preserves the integrity of the Grantor's intentions and fosters harmony among the Beneficiaries.

The Successor Trustee's First Steps: Laying the Groundwork for Trust Administration

The transition to the role of Successor Trustee marks a critical juncture in the life cycle of a Trust.

This Section outlines the essential first steps a Successor Trustee should take upon assuming their role and setting a strong foundation for effective Trust administration. The initial actions, from thoroughly reviewing the Trust document to inventorying the Trust's assets, are pivotal for aligning the Trustee's responsibilities with the Trust's objectives and the Beneficiaries' best interests.

1. Understand the Terms: Begin with a comprehensive review of the Trust document to understand its terms, including the Grantor's intentions, the identification of Beneficiaries and the specific duties and powers granted to you as the Trustee.

2. Clarify Any Ambiguities: Seek legal advice to clarify any ambiguities or complex provisions within the Trust document to ensure you fully understand the scope of your responsibilities and the Trust's objectives.

3. Inform Beneficiaries: Notify the Beneficiaries of your appointment as the Successor Trustee. This communication should be timely, respectful and informative, providing them with an overview of the Trust's status and your role.

4. Notify Financial Institutions and Advisors: Inform banks, investment firms and any financial advisors associated with the Trust of your assumption of the Trustee role. Providing formal documentation of your appointment will facilitate access to the Trust's accounts and records. Please note that the term "inform" is not a casual contact like a telephone

call. It should be in writing and always include the query if something more formal is required to notify you, in writing, immediately. Always keep a record of such contacts. Always require them to respond in writing.

5. Catalog Assets: Conduct a detailed inventory of the Trust's assets. This includes bank accounts, real estate, stocks, bonds and personal property deemed part of the Trust. Accurate valuation of these assets is crucial for effective management and reporting.

6. Secure Assets: Ensure that all assets are secure and adequately insured, if applicable. This may involve changing locks on property, updating insurance policies, and transferring asset titles to reflect the Trust's ownership.

7. Review Financial Statements: Examine the Trust's financial statements and records to assess its current financial health, including assets, liabilities, income and expenses.

8. Understand Tax Obligations: Familiarize yourself with the Trust's tax situation, including any outstanding obligations and upcoming filing requirements. Consulting a tax professional experienced with Trust taxation can be beneficial.

9. Organize Documentation: Set up a comprehensive system for documenting all actions taken, financial transactions, communications with Beneficiaries

and decisions made in your role as Trustee. This system will be invaluable for annual reporting, tax filings, potential audits, and as protection for you as a Trustee if any conflict arises.

10. Plan for Regular Updates: Establish a schedule for regular communication with Beneficiaries to update them on the Trust's status, significant actions taken and any changes affecting the Trust. Communication helps build confidence and can prevent conflicts or misunderstandings.

11. Legal and Financial Advisors: Remember, early consultation with legal and financial advisors can provide critical guidance on complex aspects of Trust administration, helping to ensure compliance with legal requirements and the prudent management of Trust assets.

12. Verify Bond Requirements: If the Trust document or state law requires you to post a fiduciary bond, take steps to secure and maintain this bond. This bond acts as an insurance policy for the Beneficiaries against potential mismanagement of the Trust's assets, as well as protects the Successor Trustee.

13. Outline Your Strategy: Based on your understanding of the Trust document and the Trust's assets and needs, develop a plan for the Trust's ongoing administration. This plan should consider the Trust's objectives, the needs of the Beneficiaries and any specific instructions detailed in the Trust document.

Assuming the role of Successor Trustee is a significant responsibility that demands careful preparation and thoughtful action. By methodically addressing these initial steps, you lay a solid foundation for a successful administration. This foundation is not just about compliance and asset management; it's about honoring the Grantor's intentions, safeguarding the Beneficiaries' interests and ensuring the Trust's objectives are met with integrity and prudence.

As you embark on this journey, remember that the role of a Successor Trustee is multifaceted. It requires a blend of diligence and foresight. The early stages of your tenure will set the tone for your relationship with the Beneficiaries and your effectiveness in managing the Trust. By taking these initial steps seriously, you demonstrate your commitment to your fiduciary duties and begin to build the confidence of all parties involved.

The complexities of Trust administration mean that challenges and questions will inevitably arise. Your willingness to consult with professionals, your proactive approach to communication and your meticulous record-keeping will serve as your best tools to navigate these challenges.

The role of a Successor Trustee is both an honor and a substantial responsibility. By carefully following these initial steps, you ensure that you are well prepared to fulfill your duties and manage the Trust to the best of your ability. Your role is crucial in ensuring the Trust achieves its purpose, providing for the Beneficiaries in accordance with the Grantor's wishes.

Navigating Complex Waters: The Successor Trustee's Guide to Professional Assistance

Assuming the role of a Successor Trustee often involves navigating complex legal, financial, and tax landscapes that can be challenging for those without specialized knowledge. This Section explores the circumstances under which a Successor Trustee might need to consult with professionals, offering guidance on how to select and work effectively with these experts to fulfill their responsibilities with confidence and diligence.

Several scenarios may necessitate the engagement of legal, financial or tax professionals. Understanding when to seek this assistance is crucial for the successful administration of the Trust.

1. Legal Complexity: The Trust document may contain provisions that are difficult to interpret or execute without legal expertise, particularly if the Trust involves multi-jurisdictional assets, complex distribution mechanisms or if disputes among Beneficiaries arise.

2. Financial Management: Professional financial advice may be required when managing and investing the Trust's assets, especially if the Trust portfolio includes complex investment vehicles, commercial ventures or real estate requiring active management.

3. Tax Obligations: Tax laws affecting Trusts can be intricate and subject to change. A tax professional's guidance is invaluable for ensuring compliance, optimizing tax strategies and handling filings, especially for high-value Trusts or those with Beneficiaries in multiple tax jurisdictions.

The choice of professionals to assist with Trust administration is as critical as the decision to seek help. The following steps can guide this selection process:

1. Look for Specialized Expertise: Focus on professionals with specific experience in Trust administration. Lawyers, accountants and financial advisors with a deep understanding of Trust law, fiduciary income tax and investment management for Trusts are more likely to provide the informed advice needed.

2. Check References and Credentials: Verify the credentials of potential advisors, including their licensure, certifications and any disciplinary history. References from clients in similar situations can provide insights into the professionals' expertise and working style.

3. Consider Compatibility: The working relationship between you and your advisors is important. Choose professionals whose communication style, availability and approach to problem-solving align with your needs and preferences.

Once you've selected your advisors, establishing

a productive working relationship is key to effectively managing the Trust. Consider the following strategies:

1. Clear Communication: Articulate your needs, expectations and any specific concerns regarding the Trust clearly. Provide comprehensive information about the Trust's assets, Beneficiaries and any known issues to enable your advisors to offer tailored advice.

2. Collaborative Decision-Making: While professionals will provide expert advice, remember that decisions regarding the Trust's administration rest with you as the Trustee. Engage in discussions, ask questions and weigh their advice carefully against the Trust's objectives and Beneficiaries' interests.

3. Ongoing Education: Use the opportunity to deepen your understanding of Trust administration. Ask your advisors to explain complex issues or the rationale behind their recommendations to enhance your ability to make informed decisions.

4. Regular Reviews: Schedule regular meetings with your advisors to review the Trust's status, discuss any changes in legal or tax landscapes and adjust strategies as necessary.

5. Document Advice and Decisions: Keep detailed records of the advice received and the decisions made based on that advice. This documentation can be crucial for demonstrating diligence and

compliance with your fiduciary duties in case of disputes or audits.

The administration of a Trust can present a myriad of challenges that may be beyond the expertise of a Successor Trustee. Recognizing when to seek professional assistance and knowing how to select and work with the right advisors are essential skills that ensure the Trust is managed efficiently, legally and in the best interests of the Beneficiaries. By leveraging the expertise of legal, financial, and tax professionals when needed, a Successor Trustee can navigate the complexities of Trust Administration with confidence, ensuring the Grantor's intentions are honored and the Beneficiaries' well-being is safeguarded.

Navigating Trust Administration: A Roadmap for Successor Trustees and Grantors

As we reach the conclusion of our exploration into the multifaceted world of Trust administration, it is clear that the roles of both the Grantor and the Successor Trustee are pivotal to the Trust's success. From the initial steps of establishing a Trust to the detailed responsibilities of managing it and the strategic considerations in selecting a Successor Trustee, each phase requires careful thought, preparation, and action. This final section synthesizes the key insights from the previous sections, offering an overview and closing thoughts on navigating the complexities of Trust administration effectively.

The journey begins with a thorough understanding of the Trust's purpose and the responsibilities it entails. For Grantors, this means considering the objectives of the Trust, the needs of the Beneficiaries and the qualities necessary in a Trustee to fulfill their vision. For Successor Trustees, it involves a deep dive into the Trust document, a clear grasp of the legal and financial duties at hand and an appreciation of the Trust's broader impact on the Beneficiaries' lives.

Effective Trust Administration is underscored by open communication and diligent management. Successor Trustees should establish regular communication channels with Beneficiaries, ensuring that all parties are informed and that any concerns are addressed promptly. Likewise, the meticulous management of Trust assets, from careful investment strategies to the prudent handling of distributions, requires both a keen understanding of financial principles and a steadfast commitment to the Trust's long-term goals. Regular, clear communication not only builds trust but also serves as a preventive measure against potential disputes or misunderstandings.

Trust Administration is not without its challenges, including navigating Beneficiary expectations and managing potential conflicts. Successor Trustees must be equipped with strategies for conflict resolution, emphasizing negotiation skills to address disputes amicably and effectively. Additionally, the ability to adapt to changing circumstances—whether legal, financial, or familial—ensures that the Trust can weather unforeseen challenges while staying true to its objectives.

For Grantors, the selection of a Successor Trustee is a decision that carries lasting implications for the Trust's administration. This choice requires a balance between personal trust, professional expertise and the potential for continuity and stability.

The landscape of Trust Administration is ever evolving, with changes in legal regulations, financial markets and family dynamics presenting ongoing learning opportunities for Successor Trustees. Embracing a mindset of continuous education and seeking professional guidance when necessary are key to navigating these changes. Professionals can offer invaluable insights into complex legal, tax, and investment matters, helping Trustees make informed decisions that benefit the Trust and its Beneficiaries.

The stewardship of a Trust is a profound responsibility, requiring a blend of knowledge, skill and compassion. For both Grantors and Successor Trustees, the journey of Trust Administration is one of commitment to the Trust's objectives, dedication to the Beneficiaries' well-being and adherence to the principles of fairness and integrity. By following the guidance outlined in this Chapter, you will be equipped to navigate the challenges and rewards of Trust Administration, ensuring that the Trust fulfills its purpose as a lasting legacy for its Beneficiaries.

Remember that the role of a Trustee is not just a legal obligation but a testament to the confidence placed in the Trustee by the Grantor and the Beneficiaries. With the right preparation, communication and approach, the administration of a Trust can be a fulfilling endeavor that honors the Grantor's intentions and secures the financial future of the Beneficiaries.

"In this world, nothing can be said to be certain, except death and taxes."
—BENJAMIN FRANKLIN

"The avoidance of taxes is the only intellectual pursuit that still carries any reward."
—JOHN MAYNARD KEYNES

"I am in favor of cutting taxes under any circumstances and for any excuse, for any reason, whenever it's possible."
—MILTON FRIEDMAN

"I am proud to be paying taxes in the United States. The only thing is — I could be just as proud for half the money."
—ARTHUR GODFREY

CHAPTER NINE

Federal Estate Tax and the AB Trust

In the landscape of estate planning, AB Trusts once stood as a cornerstone strategy for couples aiming to maximize their estate tax exemptions. These Trusts, designed to split into two upon the death of the first spouse—namely, the A (or marital) Trust and the B (or bypass) Trust—allowed couples to double the amount exempted from estate taxes. However, the passage of the Taxpayer Relief Act of 2012 marked a pivotal shift in estate planning, introducing changes that have since questioned the utility and wisdom of continuing to use AB Trusts. In fact, many lawyers believe AB Trusts to be too complicated and expensive to administer and for all practical purposes to be obsolete for their clients. They believe further that most AB Trusts that were created before 2012 were not even needed or useful at the time of their creation and often were so poorly written as not to qualify for the extended tax exemption.

At its core, an AB Trust refers to a Trust arrangement typically created by a married couple to maximize the use of their federal estate tax exemption. The name "AB Trust" derives from the Trust being split into two separate entities upon the death of the first spouse: Trust A (also known as the "Survivor's Trust," "Spouse's Trust," the "Marital Trust" or "A Trust") and Trust B (the "Bypass Trust," "Credit Shelter Trust," "Family Trust" or "B Trust"). This bifurcation is designed to take full advantage of both spouses' estate tax exemptions, potentially saving a significant amount in taxes upon the death of the surviving spouse. This Chapter explains the complex world of AB Trusts, examining their function and appeal prior to 2012. It outlines the foundational principles that made AB Trusts a prevalent choice for married couples seeking to mitigate their estate tax liabilities. As we navigate through the transformative impacts of the Taxpayer Relief Act of 2012, we uncover how the introduction of portability for the estate tax exemption between spouses has fundamentally altered the estate planning arena, rendering AB Trusts largely ineffective and for most, an unwise choice.

The critical disadvantages of maintaining an AB Trust in today's tax and legal environment are brought to light, emphasizing the urgency for individuals to reassess and revise their estate planning strategies. Despite the allure of AB Trusts in the past, the substantial changes in estate tax law post-2012 have made it clear that these Trusts now offer more limitations than benefits.

Yet the question arises: Are there any scenarios in which maintaining an AB Trust could still be beneficial? This Chapter addresses this query, providing a nuanced view that while there may be rare exceptions, the general consensus leans heavily towards the exploration of alternatives.

As we proceed, the focus shifts to the modern strategies and Trust structures that have emerged as superior alternatives to AB Trusts in light of current tax laws. These new strategies not only comply with contemporary legal standards but also offer enhanced flexibility and tax efficiency.

For individuals with existing AB Trusts, the path forward involves critical decision-making. This Chapter offers guidance on revising or replacing existing AB Trusts, aligning estate plans with contemporary best practices and navigating the complex landscape of modern estate planning with confidence and clarity.

The evolution from AB Trusts to more adaptable and tax-efficient estate planning strategies reflects the dynamic nature of law and personal finance. By thoroughly understanding the shifts prompted by the Taxpayer Relief Act of 2012 and embracing the advanced alternatives now available, individuals can ensure that their estate planning efforts are both effective and aligned with current legal standards. As you read this Chapter you may be inclined to think it unduly repeats some things even to the point of redundancy. Press forward. The repetition is purposeful in context of the particular section you are reading.

Understanding AB Trusts and Their Role in Pre-2012 Estate Planning

Before the Taxpayer Relief Act of 2012 reshaped the estate planning landscape, AB Trusts were a cornerstone strategy for married couples seeking to optimize their estate tax exemptions. This Chapter looks into the mechanics, purposes and historical significance of AB Trusts, shedding light on their function and why they were once a preferred tool for estate planning.

The functionality of AB Trusts prior to 2012 was predicated on the estate tax laws then in effect. When the first spouse died, their portion of the estate would fund Trust B up to the maximum amount allowed under the federal estate tax exemption, with the remainder going to Trust A or directly to the surviving spouse. In an effort to be thorough, it must be noted that funding the B Trust first, which of course, was necessary to take full advantage of the benefits of an AB Trust, created enormous problems for many people who were given an AB Trust by their lawyer when, in fact, their specific circumstances did not benefit from an AB

Trust. Often, the size of the estate was well within the tax exemption available without the need to use an AB Trust. In such a circumstance, using an AB Trust would sometimes effectively disinherit the surviving spouse or at least extremely limit the surviving spouse. Trust B was irrevocable, meaning it could not be altered after the first spouse's death. It provided limited resources for the surviving spouse's financial needs without being considered part of the taxable estate. Upon the surviving spouse's death, the assets in Trust B would pass to the designated Beneficiaries, often the couple's children, without being subject to federal estate taxes.

The primary advantage of utilizing an AB Trust before the Taxpayer Relief Act of 2012 was its ability to maximize the estate tax exemption for both spouses. By splitting the estate into two Trusts, a couple could effectively double the amount exempted from federal estate taxes. This was particularly beneficial in a legal environment where the individual estate tax exemption was lower and there was no portability of the exemption between spouses—meaning the unused exemption amount of the first spouse to die could not be transferred to the surviving spouse.

AB Trusts were not just about tax savings; they also allowed for a degree of control over the distribution of assets after both spouses had passed away. For example, Trust B could be structured to provide income to the surviving spouse but ensure that the principal was preserved for the next generation. This could prevent the principal from being depleted by the surviving spouse's potential remarriage or poor financial decisions. (Using the Trust for this purpose was thought by some lawyers a form of bondage for the surviving spouse or at least an expression of lack of trust.)

Prior to the Taxpayer Relief Act of 2012, AB Trusts played a pivotal role in the estate planning strategies of married couples. They offered a method to minimize estate taxes while providing for the surviving spouse and ensuring that assets were preserved for future Beneficiaries. The legal and tax environment at the time made AB Trusts a wise choice for many, highlighting the importance of understanding the interplay between estate planning tools and the prevailing tax laws. As we will explore in subsequent Sections, the landscape of estate planning has evolved significantly since the introduction of the Taxpayer Relief Act of 2012, leading to a dramatic decline in the use of AB Trusts. Many lawyers suggest an outright abandonment of using AB Trusts. However, the principles underlying these Trusts remain a testament to the adaptability and complexity of estate planning strategies.

The Evolution of Estate Planning: The Impact of the Taxpayer Relief Act of 2012 on AB Trusts

The Taxpayer Relief Act of 2012 marked a significant turning point in the landscape of estate planning in the United States, fundamentally altering the utility of AB Trusts. This Section investigates the specific changes introduced by the Act, focusing on how these modifications have shifted the strategic considerations for estate planners and Beneficiaries alike.

Before the enactment of the Taxpayer Relief Act of 2012, the estate tax exemption amount was subject to frequent changes, creating uncertainty in estate planning. AB Trusts were a popular mechanism for married couples to maximize their estate tax exemptions. By dividing the estate into two Trusts upon the first spouse's death, a couple could shield a significant portion of their wealth from estate taxes, benefiting their heirs.

The Taxpayer Relief Act of 2012 brought about pivotal changes that reshaped estate planning strategies, particularly affecting the utility of AB Trusts. The most notable changes included:

1. Permanent Estate Tax Exemption and Annual Indexing: The Act made permanent the estate tax exemption amount, setting it at $5 million per individual, adjusted annually for inflation. This provided a level of predictability and security that had been lacking, allowing individuals and couples to plan their estates with greater certainty.

2. Introduction of Portability: Perhaps the most impactful change was the introduction of portability of the estate tax exemption between spouses. This meant that the unused portion of the estate tax exemption of the first spouse to die could be

transferred to the surviving spouse, effectively doubling the amount the surviving spouse could pass on tax-free without the need for AB Trusts.

The introduction of portability significantly diminished the necessity of AB Trusts for the sole purpose of maximizing the estate tax exemption. Couples could now achieve the same tax-saving effect simply by electing portability without the need to divide assets into separate Trusts. This simplification of estate planning offered several advantages:

1. Simplicity and Flexibility: Estate planning became simpler, with less need for complex Trust structures that could be rigid and difficult to manage.

2. Direct Control for Surviving Spouses: Surviving spouses gained direct control over the entirety of the couple's assets, without the restrictions that AB Trusts could impose.

3. Reduced Costs and Complexity: The reduction in the need for AB Trusts also meant a reduction in the legal and administrative costs associated with creating and managing these Trusts.

Despite their diminished role, AB Trusts remain relevant in certain narrow situations. For estates that exceed the combined exemption amount, AB Trusts can still offer valuable tax savings. Additionally, AB Trusts can provide benefits such as asset protection from creditors, remarriage protection, and the ability to control the distribution of assets to Beneficiaries beyond the surviving spouse.

The Taxpayer Relief Act of 2012 fundamentally altered the landscape of estate tax exemptions, rendering AB Trusts less necessary for nearly all couples. By introducing portability, the Act simplified estate planning, offering greater flexibility and control to surviving spouses. However, AB Trusts continue to hold value in specific limited circumstances, underscoring the importance of tailored estate planning strategies. As the estate planning environment evolves, individuals and couples must stay informed and adaptable to ensure their estate planning objectives are met efficiently and effectively. Remaining informed seems almost impossible. The better practice is to engage an experienced lawyer who is already informed.

Rethinking AB Trusts: Navigating the Disadvantages in Contemporary Estate Planning

In the ever-evolving landscape of estate planning, the suitability of traditional tools must be critically evaluated in light of current tax laws and societal changes. AB Trusts, once a cornerstone strategy for married couples to minimize estate taxes, now present a series of critical disadvantages that necessitate a thorough reassessment. This section explores these disadvantages in greater depth, offering insights into why and how the changing legal and tax environment has impacted the efficacy of AB Trusts.

The escalation of federal estate tax exemption amounts has fundamentally altered the calculus for utilizing AB Trusts. With the exemption now significantly higher than in the past, the urgency to shield assets from estate taxes—a primary motivation for AB Trusts—has markedly decreased for the vast majority of estates. This shift not only questions the necessity of such Trusts but also highlights the importance of simplicity and adaptability in estate planning. The once-clear tax benefits of AB Trusts have been overshadowed by a tax regime that renders them redundant for most Americans, compelling a move towards more straightforward estate planning mechanisms.

The operational intricacies of AB Trusts pose significant challenges. Upon the first spouse's death, the division of assets into separate Trusts necessitates a level of administrative diligence that can be burdensome. This structure imposes constraints on the surviving spouse's access to the assets, often leading to unnecessary complexity and potential financial strain. The rigidity of AB Trusts, especially in adjusting to the surviving spouse's changing needs, underscores a critical disadvantage in an era where flexibility and ease of management are paramount.

Portability has emerged as a game-changer in estate planning, allowing a surviving spouse to utilize the deceased spouse's unused federal estate tax exemption without the need for AB Trusts. This simplification is a significant advantage that AB Trusts cannot offer, aligning more closely with the needs of modern families. By ignoring the benefits of portability, individuals risk adhering to an outdated strategy that complicates their estate planning without providing corresponding benefits.

One of the most overlooked disadvantages of maintaining an AB Trust is the potential for increased capital gains taxes. The bypass Trust does not benefit from a step-up in cost basis at the surviving spouse's death, potentially resulting in a substantial Capital Gains tax liability when heirs sell the assets. This aspect is particularly troubling in light of rising property values and can erode the financial legacy intended for heirs.

The legal and tax landscape is dynamic, with changes that can suddenly alter the effectiveness of established estate planning strategies. AB Trusts, with their inherent inflexibility, may not easily accommodate new legislative shifts or tax policy changes, potentially leading to suboptimal outcomes. This rigidity highlights the critical need for estate planning that can adapt to changing legal frameworks, ensuring that strategies remain aligned with the latest laws and best practices.

Modern families often feature complexities such as blended families, multiple marriages, and non-traditional arrangements, which AB Trusts may not adequately accommodate. The fixed nature of these Trusts can lead to unintended disinheritance or conflict among family members, suggesting a misalignment with contemporary family dynamics. The need for estate planning tools that offer customizable solutions to fit the unique structures and needs of modern families has never been more pronounced.

The landscape of estate planning is characterized by continuous change, necessitating a reevaluation of traditional strategies like AB Trusts. The critical disadvantages highlighted in this section—ranging from diminished tax benefits to operational complexity and inflexibility—underscore the need for a shift towards more adaptable and straightforward estate planning approaches. By embracing strategies that reflect the current legal and tax environment, as well as the evolving nature of family dynamics, individuals can ensure that their estate planning is both effective and aligned with their intentions. As we move forward, the importance of staying informed and adaptable in the face of legislative and societal changes will be key to achieving optimal estate planning outcomes.

Navigating the Crossroads: AB Trusts Versus Modern Alternatives in Estate Planning

In the ever-evolving landscape of estate tax law, particularly following the significant shifts initiated by the Taxpayer Relief Act of 2012, individuals and estate planners find themselves at a crossroads. The question at hand—whether there are compelling reasons to maintain an AB Trust or if it's generally wiser to consider alternatives—demands a nuanced exploration. This section aims to dissect this query, examining scenarios where an AB Trust might still hold relevance, while concurrently emphasizing the strategic advantages of modern estate planning alternatives.

The landscape post-2012 has been characterized by increased estate tax exemptions and the introduction of portability, which collectively have diminished the necessity for AB Trusts for the primary purpose of minimizing federal estate taxes. This shift necessitates a deeper understanding of the specific functions and benefits AB Trusts can still offer and under what rare circumstances they remain a viable option.

Despite the broad trend away from AB Trusts, there are nuanced scenarios where they might still serve a purpose. In jurisdictions where State estate or inheritance taxes present a significant concern, and the exemptions do not align with the generous Federal thresholds, AB Trusts can offer a strategic solution. These Trusts can help minimize the State-level tax impact, providing a compelling reason for their use in specific geographic contexts.

AB Trusts inherently offer a degree of asset protection that might be particularly appealing to individuals concerned about shielding their estate from potential creditors or legal judgments. The separation of assets into distinct Trusts under the AB Trust structure can serve as a barrier against claims, ensuring that a portion of the estate remains protected for the intended Beneficiaries. It is important to note that protection from creditors is not effective while Grantors are living. There may be more effective means to do this.

The precise control over asset distribution that AB Trusts afford can be crucial in complex family situations, such as blended families or when there are specific intentions for the inheritance beyond the surviving spouse's lifetime. The ability to dictate the terms of distribution and protect the interests of children from previous marriages or other designated heirs remains a utility of AB Trusts.

For partners in long-term committed relationships outside the legal bounds of marriage, AB Trusts can mimic some of the estate planning benefits traditionally reserved for married couples. This capability allows for creative estate planning solutions that respect the partners' wishes and provides for mutual support and inheritance strategies.

While acknowledging the scenarios where AB Trusts may still have merit, the overarching narrative leans towards the benefits of simpler, more adaptable estate planning tools. These methods adapt more readily to changes in law and personal circumstances, emphasizing direct control, ease of management and the potential for tax efficiency without the complexities and potential pitfalls associated with AB Trusts.

The decision to maintain or establish an AB Trust in the post-2012 legal environment hinges on a strategic balance between the complexity it introduces and the specific benefits it may provide under certain circumstances. For most individuals, the shift towards alternative estate planning strategies offers a path that aligns more closely with contemporary legal realities and personal estate planning goals. However, for those in unique situations where the specific advantages of AB Trusts are clear and compelling, these structures can still play a role in a comprehensive estate planning strategy.

The nuanced examination of AB Trusts versus modern alternatives reveals a landscape of estate planning that is deeply influenced by individual circumstances, legal developments and personal objectives. While the trend has moved towards simpler, more adaptable estate planning tools, the decision to utilize an AB Trust should be informed by a careful consideration of its unique benefits in specific contexts. Engaging in comprehensive estate planning, informed by current laws and personal needs, remains the cornerstone of effectively navigating this complex domain, ensuring that estate planning strategies are both effective and aligned with the evolving landscape.

Beyond AB Trusts: Superior Estate Planning Strategies in the Modern Tax Era

The evolution of tax laws, especially since the Taxpayer Relief Act of 2012, has significantly altered the landscape of estate planning. With these changes, a variety of estate planning strategies and Trust structures have emerged, offering more flexible, tax-efficient and simpler alternatives to the traditional AB Trust. This section explores these superior alternatives, highlighting how they align with contemporary needs and offering a roadmap for individuals seeking to navigate the complexities of modern estate planning effectively.

Revocable Living Trusts have gained popularity as a versatile estate planning tool, offering several advantages over AB Trusts. Unlike AB Trusts, which in part become irrevocable upon the death of one spouse, Revocable Living Trusts allow for adjustments during the Grantor's lifetime. This flexibility is crucial in adapting to changes in laws or personal circumstances. Moreover, Revocable Living Trusts facilitate a smoother transfer of assets upon death by avoiding the time-consuming and costly probate process.

The portability election, a direct outcome of recent tax law changes, allows a surviving spouse to use any unused Federal Estate and Gift Tax Exemption of the deceased spouse. This simplification of estate tax planning effectively doubles the exemption amount a married couple can transfer tax-free without the need for complex Trust structures. Portability has made estate planning more straightforward for many couples, rendering the traditional AB Trust structure unnecessary for tax avoidance purposes.

Disclaimer Trusts offer an alternative that retains the flexibility often missing in AB Trust arrangements. Upon the first spouse's death, the surviving spouse has the option (usually within nine months) to disclaim (refuse) part of the inheritance, directing it into the Trust. This strategy allows for postmortem planning based on the family's current financial situation and tax laws, providing a level of adaptability that is particularly valuable in a rapidly changing legal landscape.

Irrevocable Life Insurance Trusts (ILITs) have emerged as a strategic tool for managing estate taxes related to life insurance proceeds. By holding a life insurance policy within an ILIT, the death benefit can be excluded from the estate, preventing it from contributing to the estate's overall value for tax purposes. This approach is especially beneficial for individuals with significant assets in life insurance, offering a path to preserve more wealth for Beneficiaries.

Several Trust structures cater to specific goals or situations, offering advantages in the right contexts:

1. Charitable Remainder Trusts (CRTs): CRTs provide a way to donate to charity while receiving income during the Grantor's lifetime, offering tax benefits and fulfilling philanthropic goals.

2. Qualified Personal Residence Trusts (QPRTs): For individuals seeking to transfer a primary residence or vacation home to their heirs, QPRTs offer a tax-efficient method to reduce the estate's value.

3. Grantor Retained Annuity Trusts (GRATs): GRATs allow the transfer of asset growth out of an estate while the Grantor retains an income stream, useful

for assets expected to appreciate significantly.

The advancements in estate planning strategies and the development of Trust structures beyond the AB Trust reflect a broader trend towards flexibility, tax efficiency and simplicity. These alternatives offer tailored solutions that can better meet the diverse needs of individuals in the modern tax era. By understanding and leveraging these superior options, estate planners and individuals can craft estate plans that not only comply with current laws but also provide for the efficient transfer of wealth according to their wishes, ensuring a legacy that reflects their values and goals.

Modernizing Legacy Estate Plans: Transitioning Away from AB Trusts

In the wake of substantial changes in estate tax law and the evolution of family structures, individuals with existing AB Trusts face a crucial juncture. The necessity to revise or replace their estate plans to align with contemporary best practices is not merely advisable but essential for ensuring that their estate planning objectives are met efficiently and effectively. This section outlines the critical steps for individuals to consider as they navigate the process of modernizing their estate plans, moving away from AB Trusts to embrace more flexible and tax-efficient strategies.

The first step in modernizing an estate plan involves a thorough review of the existing documents and structures, with a particular focus on the objectives and provisions of the AB Trust. This review should assess how current laws affect the Trust's tax efficiency and its alignment with the Grantor's estate planning goals, especially considering the increased Federal Estate Tax Exemptions and the introduction of portability.

Given the complexity of estate planning and the nuanced changes in law, consulting with estate planning professionals—such as attorneys, tax advisors and financial planners—is crucial. These experts can provide valuable insights into the implications of maintaining an AB Trust, offer guidance on modern estate planning strategies and help devise a plan that aligns with current best practices while meeting the individual's specific needs.

Individuals should consider their need for flexibility and control over their assets. This evaluation will help determine whether transitioning to alternatives like Revocable Living Trusts, which offer more control and easier management during the Grantor's lifetime, would be beneficial. Such Trusts also allow for seamless updates to the estate plan as laws and personal circumstances change, providing a level of adaptability AB Trusts cannot.

For married individuals, understanding the impact of portability on their estate planning strategy is imperative. Evaluating whether the simplicity and efficiency of utilizing portability for the unused estate tax exemption amount suits their needs better than the complexities of an AB Trust is a critical consideration.

This step involves analyzing the potential tax implications and the ease of transferring assets to the surviving spouse and other beneficiaries.

Exploring alternative Trust structures tailored to specific goals—such as ILITs for life insurance proceeds, CRTs for charitable giving, or GRATs for transferring asset appreciation—is an essential step. These alternatives can offer targeted solutions for tax efficiency, asset protection, and charitable intentions, providing a more customized approach to estate planning.

After deciding on a revised estate plan, the implementation process involves executing new estate planning documents and possibly dissolving the AB Trust, subject to professional advice. This step is crucial for ensuring that the estate plan reflects the individual's current wishes and the latest legal standards. Continuous review of the estate plan, after significant life events or legal changes, ensures that the plan remains aligned with the individual's goals and adapts to evolving best practices.

Transitioning away from AB Trusts and modernizing legacy estate plans is a necessary step for many individuals to ensure their estate planning strategy reflects current best practices. By following these critical steps and leveraging professional advice, individuals can navigate the complexities of this transition, ensuring their estate plans are flexible, tax-efficient and aligned with their objectives. The evolution from AB Trusts to more adaptable estate planning strategies underscores the importance of proactive engagement with one's estate planning in the face of legal and personal change.

Navigating New Horizons in Estate Planning: Preferred Alternatives to AB Trusts Post-2012

As repeatedly stated in this Chapter, the landscape of estate planning has undergone significant transformation since the Taxpayer Relief Act of 2012, prompting individuals and estate planners to seek alternatives to traditional AB Trusts. With the increase in federal estate tax exemptions and the introduction of portability, new strategies have emerged as more effective tools for managing estate plans in alignment with current tax laws. This section touches on these alternatives, highlighting the advantages they offer and how they have come to be preferred options for estate planning in the modern legal environment.

One of the notable shifts in estate planning strategies post-2012 is the increasing use of standalone Survivor's Trusts. This approach involves creating a single Trust for the surviving spouse, which can be structured to provide benefits similar to those of an AB Trust but with greater flexibility and simplicity. Unlike AB Trusts, which require splitting assets upon the first spouse's death, a standalone Survivor's Trust allows for continuous management of the assets under one Trust, simplifying administration and potentially reducing management costs.

The portability election has become a cornerstone of modern estate planning, allowing a surviving spouse to utilize any unused portion of their deceased spouse's federal estate and gift tax exemption. This simplification eliminates the need for the complex structuring inherent in AB Trusts, offering a more straightforward path to minimizing estate taxes. Portability provides couples with the flexibility to pass on wealth without engaging in the meticulous splitting of assets, making it a preferred strategy for its ease of use and effectiveness in tax planning.

Revocable Living Trusts have gained popularity as a versatile alternative to AB Trusts, offering individuals control over their assets during their lifetime with the ability to amend or revoke the Trust as needed. This flexibility is particularly appealing in an ever-changing legal landscape, allowing for adjustments in response to new laws or personal circumstances. Additionally, Revocable Living Trusts facilitate the seamless transfer of assets upon death, avoiding the Probate process and providing a clear, efficient mechanism for asset distribution.

A critical aspect of embracing alternatives to AB Trusts is the recognition that estate planning is an ongoing process. Regular reviews and adjustments ensure that estate plans remain aligned with current laws, tax regulations, and the individual's evolving goals. This proactive approach allows individuals to capitalize on new opportunities and strategies that may arise as legal and tax environments evolve.

The shift away from AB Trusts toward these emerging strategies reflects a broader trend in estate planning towards simplicity, flexibility and tax efficiency. Standalone Survivor's Trusts, the strategic use of portability, Revocable Living Trusts, and specialized Trusts for targeted objectives offer compelling alternatives for individuals looking to navigate the complexities of estate planning in today's legal landscape. By understanding and leveraging these preferred strategies, estate planners and individuals can ensure that their estate planning efforts are both effective and aligned with the best practices of the modern era.

Embracing Change in Estate Planning Strategies

The evolution of estate planning, particularly in the wake of the Taxpayer Relief Act of 2012 and subsequent legal and tax developments, represents a significant shift in how individuals should approach the management and distribution of their estates. Through the sections addressing these critical changes, we have navigated the complexities of transitioning from traditional AB Trusts to more contemporary and flexible estate planning strategies. This journey underscores the importance of adaptability and proactive planning in the face of legal evolutions.

The critical examination of AB Trusts and the exploration of modern alternatives highlight a broader theme: the necessity for estate plans to evolve alongside changes in law and personal circumstances. The emergence of standalone Survivor's Trusts, the strategic use of portability, Revocable Living Trusts, and specialized Trusts for targeted goals underscore the diverse tools available to individuals seeking to optimize their estate planning in today's legal landscape.

Moreover, the guidance provided for individuals with existing AB Trusts—ranging from conducting thorough reviews of current estate plans to consulting with professionals and considering the conversion to more adaptable Trust structures—offers a practical roadmap for aligning estate planning strategies with contemporary best practices. These steps emphasize the importance of informed decision-making and the value of expert advice in navigating the complexities of estate and tax law.

The discussion of alternatives to AB Trusts and the detailed exploration of preferred strategies in light of current tax laws further illuminate the path forward. It is clear that flexibility, control and tax efficiency have become paramount in effective estate planning. By embracing these principles and the tools that facilitate them, individuals can craft estate plans that not only comply with current regulations but also reflect their wishes and goals more accurately and efficiently.

The transition from AB Trusts to modern estate planning strategies is not merely a reaction to legislative changes but a proactive step toward securing a legacy that aligns with the Grantor's intentions and the Beneficiaries' needs. This Chapter provides an overview of this transition, offering insights and practical advice for navigating the evolving estate planning landscape. As laws and family dynamics continue to change, the principles of adaptability, informed decision-making, and continuous review remain central to achieving estate planning objectives that resonate with contemporary best practices.

"To neglect the preparation of a Will is to refuse to see the fact of death, which is the most fundamental fact of human life."
—FELIX FRANKFURTER

"If thou art rich, thou'rt poor; For, like an ass whose back with ingots bows, Thou bear'st thy heavy riches but a journey, and death unloads thee."
—SHAKESPEARE

CHAPTER TEN

Pour-Over Wills in the Trust Centered Estate Plan

In the world of estate planning, the objective is not only to ensure the orderly transfer of assets posthumously but also to do so with an eye toward privacy, efficiency, and the minimization of legal entanglements. At the heart of this endeavor lies the Trust Centered Estate Plan—the comprehensive approach that leverages the strengths of both Wills and Trusts to achieve a seamless transition of one's legacy. Among the suite of instruments that make up this plan, the Pour-Over Will stands out for its unique role and strategic importance.

This Chapter considers the Pour-Over Will, a document that, while often operating in the shadow of more prominently discussed estate planning tools, plays a necessary role in the modern estate plan. The foundational purpose of a Will in estate planning sets the stage for our exploration, establishing the traditional expectations and roles that Wills fulfill. Against this backdrop, the Pour-Over Will emerges not as a mere alternative but as a sophisticated strategy designed to enhance and complete a Trust Centered Estate Plan. Its integration with a Living Trust is not just a matter of formality but a deliberate choice to ensure that no asset is left behind, regardless of its nature or the circumstances of its ownership.

As we dissect the operational mechanics of the Pour-Over Will, we uncover its distinctive function in comparison to traditional Wills. This instrument does not merely distribute assets; it acts as a conduit, channeling them into a pre-established Living Trust with precision and purpose. This process, while appearing straightforward, involves nuanced legal and procedural steps, each of which is essential for the Pour-Over Will to fulfill its role effectively.

The precautionary and backup functions of the Pour-Over Will within a Trust Centered Estate Plan are of particular interest. These functions not only safeguard against the unintended exclusion of assets from the Trust but also serve as a testament to the thoroughness and foresight that characterizes diligent estate planning. However, despite its critical importance, the Pour-Over Will is often perceived as a document of last resort. This Chapter explores the factors contributing to its infrequent use and the circumstances under which its provisions might be activated, shedding light on the practical realities of estate execution.

By the end of this Chapter, you will have gained an understanding of the Pour-Over Will's strategic value within a Trust Centered Estate Plan, equipped with the knowledge to appreciate its nuances and the insight to apply its principles effectively in your own estate planning endeavors.

The Harmonious Integration of a Pour-Over Will into Trust Centered Estate Planning

The foundational purpose of a Will in estate planning is to ensure that a person's wishes regarding the distribution of their estate are honored after their death. A Will is a legally binding document that outlines how one's assets should be distributed among Beneficiaries, appoints guardians for minor children and may nominate an executor to manage the estate until its final distribution. The essence of a Will lies in its capacity to provide clarity, prevent potential conflicts among heirs and mitigate the risk of the estate passing according to the State's intestacy laws, which apply in the absence of a Will.

However, the traditional Will has limitations, notably its public nature due to the Probate process, potential for challenges and the time and expense involved. In response to these limitations, estate planning has evolved to include more sophisticated tools, such as Living Trusts and Pour-Over Wills, to create a more comprehensive and secure estate plan, known as a Trust Centered Estate Plan.

A Living Trust, or Revocable Trust, is a legal entity created during a person's lifetime to own and manage assets. The Trust is "living" because it is established while the Grantor (the person who creates the Trust) is alive and "revocable" because the Grantor retains the right to modify or terminate the Trust at any time. The primary advantage of a Living Trust is its ability to bypass the Probate process, thus maintaining privacy, reducing administrative costs and ensuring a smoother and quicker distribution of assets to Beneficiaries. Furthermore, it offers the flexibility of management continuity in the event of the Grantor's incapacity before death.

Enter the Pour-Over Will, a specialized type of Will designed to work in tandem with a Living Trust. The distinctive feature of a Pour-Over Will is that it names the Living Trust as the primary Beneficiary of any assets not already placed in the Trust at the time of the Grantor's death. Essentially, it "pours" any remaining assets into the Trust, ensuring that these assets are distributed according to the terms set forth in the Trust agreement, rather than under the potentially less desirable terms of a Will or State intestacy laws.

The integration of a Pour-Over Will into a Trust

Centered Estate Plan enhances the plan's effectiveness and efficiency in several ways:

1. Completeness and Cohesion: It acts as a safety net, capturing any assets inadvertently left out of the Living Trust, thus ensuring that all of the Grantor's assets are distributed in a unified manner according to the comprehensive plan laid out in the Trust.

2. Simplicity and Uniformity: By funneling all assets into the Living Trust, the Pour-Over Will simplifies the estate's administration after death. This uniformity eliminates the need to manage separate distributions under potentially conflicting directives, thus reducing the risk of legal challenges and family disputes.

3. Flexibility and Control: The Pour-Over Will, in conjunction with a Living Trust, allows for greater flexibility in estate management and control over the distribution of assets, including provisions for minor Beneficiaries, Special Needs Trusts, or charitable donations, which might be more cumbersome or less secure under a traditional Will alone.

4. Privacy and Probate Avoidance: Although the Pour-Over Will itself must go through Probate, once assets are transferred to the Living Trust, they are distributed outside of Probate, thus maintaining the privacy of the estate, and reducing time and costs associated with Probate administration.

The Pour-Over Will is not merely an ancillary document to a Living Trust; it is a critical component of a Trust Centered Estate Plan, designed to ensure that all of an individual's assets are seamlessly integrated into the estate plan, providing a comprehensive, efficient and secure method of fulfilling their final wishes. This harmonious integration underscores the evolution of estate planning from simple Wills to sophisticated arrangements that offer enhanced control, privacy and peace of mind for both the Grantor and their Beneficiaries.

The Safety Net: Pour-Over Wills in Trust Centered Estate Planning

A Pour-Over Will is uniquely designed to complement a Living Trust by ensuring that all of the Grantor's assets, even those not explicitly included in the Trust documentation, are eventually transferred to the Trust upon the Grantor's death. This precautionary function addresses the reality that despite the best efforts and intentions, significant assets may be inadvertently omitted from a Living Trust. Reasons for such omissions can vary widely, from simple oversight to the acquisition of new assets post-Trust establishment that the Grantor neglects to add to the Trust.

The Pour-Over Will acts as a catch-all mechanism, directing that any assets outside the Trust at the time of the Grantor's death be "poured over" into the Trust.

This ensures that these assets are distributed according to the Trust's terms, maintaining the integrity of the estate plan and preventing the assets from being distributed under the State's intestacy laws, which may not align with the Grantor's wishes.

Beyond its precautionary role, the Pour-Over Will serves several backup functions that enhance the resilience and comprehensiveness of a Trust Centered Estate Plan:

1. Legal Validation: It provides a legal framework for transferring assets that were not previously funded into the Trust, ensuring that the transfer process is recognized and enforced by the Courts.

2. Comprehensive Coverage: The Pour-Over Will ensures that all assets, regardless of their nature or how they were acquired, can be included in the Trust's distribution plan. This includes tangible personal property, digital assets or other forms of ownership that may not have been initially considered or that have specific title transfer requirements

3. Flexibility in Estate Management: It allows for flexibility in managing the estate, accommodating changes in the Grantor's asset portfolio without the need for constant updates to the Trust documentation. This flexibility is particularly valuable in dynamic financial environments or for individuals with complex asset structures.

The Pour-Over Will: A Document of Last Resort in Trust Centered Estate Planning

Several factors contribute to the Pour-Over Will's status as a seldom-used component of estate planning, including:

1. Proactive Trust Funding: The primary aim of a Trust Centered Estate Plan is to proactively fund the Living Trust with the Grantor's assets during their lifetime. This direct transfer of assets into the Trust circumvents the need for a Pour-Over Will since ideally, no significant assets remain outside the Trust at the time of the Grantor's death.

2. Administrative Complexity and Costs: Activation of the Pour-Over Will necessitates a Probate process for the assets it captures. This process can be time-consuming, public and potentially costly, undermining some of the key benefits of a Trust, such as privacy and expedience in asset distribution.

3. Comprehensive Estate Planning: Many individuals who establish a Trust Centered Estate Plan do so with thorough legal guidance, ensuring that all assets are correctly titled in the Trust from the outset. Such comprehensive planning efforts reduce the likelihood of oversight, thereby diminishing the need to rely on the Pour-Over Will.

Despite the intention for a Trust to fully encapsulate an individual's assets, certain circumstances may necessitate the enactment of the Pour-Over Will's provisions:

1. Acquisition of New Assets: If the Grantor acquires new assets and passes away before these assets can be titled to the Trust, the Pour-Over Will serves as a critical mechanism to ensure these assets are ultimately governed by the Trust's terms.

2. Overlooked Assets: In complex estates or situations where the Grantor has diverse holdings, some assets may inadvertently be left out of the Trust. The Pour-Over Will captures these overlooked assets, ensuring they are distributed according to the Grantor's overall estate planning intentions.

3. Intentional Retention of Personal Assets: In some cases, a Grantor may choose to retain personal assets outside the Trust for various reasons, such as simplicity or personal preference. Upon their death, the Pour-Over Will ensures these assets are funneled into the Trust for distribution.

4. Legal Challenges or Title Issues: Occasionally, assets believed to be part of the Trust may face legal challenges or issues with title clarity. The Pour-Over Will acts as a fallback to assert the Grantor's intent that such assets be part of the Trust estate.

While the Pour-Over Will is designed as a safety measure, its activation is not without implications:

1. Probate Process: Assets transferred via the Pour-Over Will undergo Probate, potentially delaying distribution and incurring additional costs.

2. Public Scrutiny: Unlike assets distributed directly

through a Trust, those passing through Probate become a matter of public record, diminishing the privacy benefit of a Trust.

3. Efficiency Concerns: The efficiency of asset distribution can be compromised, as the Probate process may introduce complexities and delays not present in Trust administration.

Supplemental Analysis: Navigating the Complexities of Pour-Over Wills in Trust Centered Estate Plans

Pour-Over Wills, integral to Trust Centered Estate Plans, offer a strategic approach to estate planning, ensuring a seamless transfer of assets into a Living Trust upon the Grantor's death. While the primary utility of these documents is well-established, their broader implications, practical considerations, and strategic nuances warrant a deeper examination.

The tax ramifications of utilizing a Pour-Over Will, in comparison to direct bequests through a traditional Will, are multifaceted. Assets transferred via a Pour-Over Will into a Living Trust may still be subject to estate taxes; however, the structured approach of a Trust can offer more sophisticated mechanisms for tax planning and minimization. For instance, Trusts can be designed to maximize the benefits of estate tax exemptions and marital deductions, potentially offering a more tax-efficient transfer of wealth than direct bequests under a traditional Will. Estate planners must carefully consider these tax implications, tailoring strategies to optimize the fiscal outcomes for the estate and its beneficiaries.

One of the compelling advantages of a Trust Centered Estate Plan, including a Pour-Over Will, is the enhanced privacy it offers. Unlike traditional Wills, which become public records through the Probate process, a Living Trust allows for the private administration of assets. The Pour-Over Will, while subject to Probate, serves primarily to transfer overlooked assets into the Trust, minimizing the extent of public exposure. This aspect is crucial for individuals who value privacy regarding the distribution of their estate.

The enforceability and effectiveness of Pour-Over Wills are significantly influenced by State law, which can vary widely. Some jurisdictions may have specific requirements or limitations regarding the use of Pour-Over Wills and Living Trusts, impacting how these estate planning tools are drafted and implemented. Estate planners must navigate these legal landscapes adeptly, ensuring that Pour-Over Wills are crafted in compliance with local laws to maintain their validity and intended function.

Pour-Over Wills play a critical role in dealing with complex assets, business interests, or international holdings within an estate. The process of transferring such assets into a Trust via a Pour-Over Will requires meticulous planning and foresight. For example, business interests may necessitate particular considerations regarding continuity and control, while international assets may involve cross-jurisdictional legal complexities. A strategic approach, considering these complexities, ensures that all assets are effectively integrated into the Trust, preserving their value and aligning with the Grantor's wishes.

The decision to incorporate a Pour-Over Will into an estate plan is nuanced, requiring a thoughtful evaluation of individual circumstances, estate objectives and family dynamics. Individuals should consider the nature of their assets, their privacy preferences, potential tax implications, and the legal environment of their jurisdiction. Consulting with estate planning professionals can provide valuable insights and guidance, aiding in the formulation of a comprehensive, tailored estate planning strategy that reflects the Grantor's goals and priorities.

While Pour-Over Wills are a powerful tool in Trust Centered Estate Plans, they are not without their challenges. The Probate process for the assets passing through the Pour-Over Will can introduce delays and additional costs, potentially complicating the estate settlement. Proactively addressing these concerns involves thorough documentation, the strategic titling of assets to ensure they are included in the Trust where possible and the consideration of alternative mechanisms for transferring certain types of assets.

Synthesizing the Pour-Over Will within Trust Centered Estate Planning

The journey through the intricacies of the Pour-Over Will within the framework of Trust Centered Estate Planning reveals a nuanced understanding of its critical role, operational mechanics, precautionary functions and procedural distinctions. This Chapter has examined the legal principles and practical applications that distinguish the Pour-Over Will not only as a pivotal estate planning instrument but also as a testament to the evolution of estate management strategies aimed at achieving comprehensive asset control, privacy and efficient distribution.

The foundational premise of the Pour-Over Will, as explored, lies in its ability to act as a safety net, ensuring that all assets, whether inadvertently left out of the Trust or acquired too close to the Grantor's passing, are ultimately governed by the Trust's terms. This mechanism provides not just a catch-all solution to potential oversights but underscores the importance of a meticulous, all-encompassing approach to estate planning that anticipates the unpredictable nature of asset acquisition and retention.

The operational dynamics of the Pour-Over Will, set against the backdrop of traditional estate planning instruments, highlight its unique position in ensuring that the estate administration process aligns with the Grantor's wishes. By effectively funneling assets into the

Trust posthumously, the Pour-Over Will streamlines the distribution process, mitigating the complexities and delays associated with Probate and reinforcing the Grantor's estate planning objectives.

The exploration of the Pour-Over Will's precautionary and backup functions further emphasizes its role in safeguarding the estate against oversights in asset inclusion. This critical analysis illuminates the Pour-Over Will's capacity to address unforeseen challenges, ensuring that the estate plan remains resilient and responsive to the dynamics of asset management and distribution.

The comparative analysis of the Pour-Over Will against traditional Wills and Trusts underscores its innovative approach to estate planning. This comparison reveals the Pour-Over Will's advantages in terms of privacy, efficiency and coherence in estate administration, providing a compelling argument for its inclusion in a Trust Centered Estate Plan.

The Pour-Over Will emerges as a cornerstone of modern estate planning, embodying the principles of foresight, flexibility, and comprehensive asset management. Its integration into a Trust Centered Estate Plan not only enhances the plan's effectiveness but also reflects a deep commitment to honoring the Grantor's wishes with the utmost fidelity and efficiency. As estate planning continues to evolve, the Pour-Over Will stands as a testament to the enduring pursuit of innovative solutions that prioritize the seamless transition of assets, the preservation of legacy and the peace of mind for both the Grantor and their Beneficiaries.

"Do something today that your future self will thank you for."
— SEAN PATRICK FLANERY

"As for the future, your task is not to foresee it, but to enable it."
— ANTOINE DE SAINT- EXUPÉRY

"Planning is bringing the future into the present so that you can do something about it now."
— ALAN LAKEIN

CHAPTER ELEVEN

Navigating Healthcare Directives

In the interplay between healthcare decisions and estate planning, Advanced Healthcare Directives (AHDs), Do Not Resuscitate (DNRs) orders and Physician Orders for Life Sustaining Treatment (POLSTs) are crucial legal tools. These instruments ensure that individual's healthcare preferences are respected, particularly in moments when they will not be able to communicate their wishes. This Chapter probes the complexities of integrating such healthcare directives into Trust Centered Estate Plans, offering an exploration of the legal, practical and ethical considerations that shape their use.

1. The Living Will details specific medical treatments an individual wishes to accept or refuse under

certain conditions, including life-sustaining measures and palliative care options. The Advanced Healthcare Directive enables the designation of a trusted individual as a healthcare proxy or agent. This agent is empowered to make healthcare decisions on behalf of the individual, adhering to the preferences outlined in their AHD. These two documents are conceptually different but are often combined into one document which we will refer to as an Advanced Healthcare Directive.

2. DNRs inform medical personnel that an individual does not wish to undergo CPR or advanced cardiac life support if their heart stops or they stop breathing.

3. POLSTs provide detailed, doctor-ordered instructions to ensure that, in an emergency, a patient receives the treatment they prefer, especially aimed at individuals with serious illnesses.

The evolving landscape of healthcare laws and patient rights necessitates a nuanced understanding of how AHDs, DNRs and POLSTs function within estate planning. We will examine the legal frameworks governing these directives, their practical implications in estate planning and the future considerations for individuals and legal practitioners alike. This Chapter provides an in-depth look at the intersection of healthcare decision-making and estate planning.

We begin by exploring the key components of AHDs, DNRs and POLSTs, and how they integrate into Trust Centered Estate Plans, reflecting on the decision-making authority of Trustees and Beneficiaries in healthcare matters. State-specific statutes influence the drafting, interpretation and enforcement of these directives, underscoring the variability and legal nuances across jurisdictions.

Moreover, we address the future considerations for integrating these directives into estate plans, considering the evolving nature of healthcare laws, the advancement of digital healthcare records, and the growing emphasis on patient autonomy and rights. This forward-looking perspective prepares individuals and legal practitioners to navigate the changing landscape of healthcare planning and estate management.

This Chapter aims to equip you with the knowledge and insights needed to make informed decisions about incorporating Advanced Healthcare Directives into your estate plan. By understanding the legal principles, practical applications, and future trends, individuals can ensure that their healthcare preferences are honored, providing peace of mind for themselves and their loved ones in the process. Please note that we use the terms "Advanced Healthcare Directives," primarily as it is defined in number "1" above. However, it is also used in this Chapter to refer collectively to all three—AHDs, DNRs and POLSTs.

Advanced Healthcare Directives in Trust Centered Estate Planning

Advanced Healthcare Directives are integral components of Trust Centered Estate Planning, crucial for ensuring that an individual's healthcare preferences are honored, particularly when they are unable to communicate their wishes. These directives bridge the gap between personal healthcare decisions and legal documentation, encompassing AHDs, DNRs and POLSTs.

The incorporation of one or more of these into estate plans is a complex process that must account for the legal variances between States, which can affect how these documents are created, witnessed, and implemented. This underscores the importance of tailoring estate planning to both the individual's healthcare wishes and the legal requirements of their State of residence.

A comprehensive estate plan that includes one or more of these and a Trust provides detailed guidance on managing an individual's assets and healthcare decisions in a coordinated manner. This not only addresses the financial aspects of estate planning but also the deeply personal choices related to healthcare.

The effectiveness of AHDs within an estate plan is contingent upon clear communication and understanding between the individual, their healthcare providers, family members and appointed agents.

It is essential to discuss and document healthcare preferences thoroughly within the estate plan to ensure that these wishes are understood and respected.

Furthermore, as circumstances and preferences evolve, so too should the AHDs within an estate plan. Regular reviews and updates are crucial to maintain alignment with the individual's current healthcare wishes and legal standards.

The strategic inclusion of AHDs in Trust Centered Estate Plans offers a holistic approach to estate planning. It marries the management of financial assets with the critical considerations of healthcare preferences, ensuring that an individual's wishes are respected and clearly communicated. By addressing the key components of AHDs and understanding their legal implications, individuals can craft estate plans that truly reflect their values, providing peace of mind and clarity for themselves and their loved ones.

The Intersection and Divergence of AHDs, DNRs and POLSTs

The concepts of AHDs, DNRs and POLSTs orders are central to the discourse on patient autonomy and end-of-life care. While these instruments share the common goal of respecting and implementing an individual's healthcare preferences, they serve distinct purposes and are governed by different legal requirements.

AHDs allow individuals to document their preferences for future medical treatment in the event they become unable to communicate their wishes. A Living Will typically outlines the types of medical interventions a person would or would not want, especially concerning life-sustaining treatment. AHDs appoint a trusted person to make healthcare decisions on behalf of the individual. In many jurisdictions these are combined into one document.

Legal Framework: Similar to POLST, the legal requirements for AHDs vary by State. Generally, these documents must be completed by the individual while they are of sound mind. While notarization is not always required, witnesses are often necessary to validate the document. Unlike POLST, which is a medical order, AHDs are legal documents that do not require a physician's signature but must be respected by healthcare providers.

DNRs are specific medical orders that instruct healthcare providers not to perform cardiopulmonary resuscitation (CPR) in the event a patient's breathing or heart stops. DNR orders are used both in hospital settings and in the community.

Legal Framework: The process for establishing a DNR varies by jurisdiction but generally involves a conversation between the patient (or their designated decision-maker) and a healthcare provider. The order is then documented in the patient's medical record. In some states, DNR orders can be included in POLST forms or AHDs, but the specificity and authority of a stand-alone DNR order are crucial for its effectiveness in emergency situations.

A POLST is a medical order that translates a patient's preferences regarding life-sustaining treatment into actionable medical orders. It is designed for individuals facing serious illness or at the end of life, where the need for these decisions is immediate. A POLST specifies the types of medical treatment that a patient wishes to receive or avoid, including resuscitation, mechanical ventilation, artificial nutrition and hydration.

Legal Framework: The POLST framework is legislated at the State level, with each State having its own version and name for the form. The form must be completed and signed by a healthcare provider, reflecting a detailed conversation between the provider and the patient or their legally recognized decision-maker. The completed POLST form is intended to be honored across healthcare settings, from emergency medical services to hospitals and long-term care facilities.

While AHDs, DNRs and POLSTs share the aim of honoring patient autonomy, they differ in their scope, implementation, and legal basis. AHDs are preventive legal documents that articulate general wishes regarding treatment preferences and designate decision-making authority, intended for use before a medical crisis occurs. DNRs are narrowly focused medical orders that apply to situations of cardiac or respiratory arrest. POLSTs are medical orders that provide specific instructions for immediate use across healthcare settings, aimed at individuals with serious illnesses or at the end of life.

Understanding the nuances between these tools is critical for healthcare professionals, legal practitioners and individuals engaging in healthcare planning. Each instrument plays a vital role in ensuring that patients receive care that aligns with their values and preferences, highlighting the importance of informed decision-making and clear communication in healthcare settings.

Choosing Among AHDs, DNRs and POLST in Estate Planning

The choice to use an AHD, DNR and POLST can significantly reflect an individual's approach to personal healthcare planning, depending on their health status, personal values and the specifics of their estate plan.

1. Imminent Health Concerns: For individuals with serious illnesses or those at an advanced stage of life, a POLST form is particularly relevant. This medical order is designed for use in situations where the patient's health condition is precarious and there is a need for immediate, actionable orders regarding life-sustaining treatments.

The POLST ensures that the patient's wishes are followed by all healthcare providers, across settings, without the need for interpretation or delays.

2. Specific Instructions Regarding Resuscitation: In cases where an individual has strong preferences against attempts at resuscitation in the event of cardiac or respiratory arrest, a DNR order is a direct and effective way to communicate this choice. This is especially pertinent for patients with terminal illnesses or those who wish to avoid aggressive life-sustaining measures that may not improve their quality of life.

Incorporating a DNR or POLST into one's estate plan showcases a proactive approach to healthcare planning. It reflects an individual's desire to retain control over their medical treatment at the end of life and to ensure that their healthcare choices are in alignment with their values and wishes.

While AHDs are broader and more encompassing, they serve a slightly different purpose than a DNR or POLST. AHDs allow individuals to outline their general healthcare preferences and appoint a healthcare proxy in situations where they might be unable to make decisions themselves. These documents are crucial for anyone looking to establish a comprehensive healthcare plan, regardless of their current health status.

A Trust Centered Estate Plan goes beyond asset

distribution, incorporating elements of healthcare planning to ensure a holistic approach to estate management. By choosing to integrate a DNR or POLST into their estate plan, an individual underscores the importance of having specific, actionable healthcare orders in place that reflect their end-of-life care preferences. This decision not only affects the individual's medical care but also has implications for how their Trustees and healthcare proxies carry out their responsibilities, aligning medical decisions with the broader goals and values outlined in their estate plan.

The choice among an AHD, DNR and POLST is deeply personal and reflects an individual's health status, values, and desires for their end-of-life care. By thoughtfully considering these options and integrating them into a Trust Centered Estate Plan, individuals can ensure that their healthcare wishes are clearly communicated and respected, providing peace of mind for themselves and their loved ones. This strategic approach to estate and healthcare planning empowers individuals to maintain control over their medical care and ensures that their estate plan is a true reflection of their personal values and wishes.

Incorporating an AHD into a Trust Centered Estate Plan has significant legal and practical implications, particularly in relation to the decision-making authority of Trustees and Beneficiaries regarding healthcare matters. This integration is not only a reflection of an individual's healthcare preferences but also a strategic approach to ensuring those preferences are respected within the broader context of estate management.

Legal Considerations

1. Authority and Autonomy: AHDs legally empower designated agents to make healthcare decisions on behalf of the individual should they become incapacitated. This clear delineation of authority ensures that the individual's healthcare preferences are followed, potentially superseding decisions that might otherwise be made by Trustees or Beneficiaries who do not have this designated authority.

2. State-Specific Regulations: The legal standing and requirements for AHDs vary by State, impacting how they are integrated into estate plans. Trustees and Beneficiaries must be aware of these nuances to ensure that the AHD is both legally valid and effectively executed in accordance with State laws.

3. Compliance with Healthcare Laws: Incorporating an AHD into an estate plan requires adherence to healthcare privacy and consent laws, such as the Health Insurance Portability and Accountability Act (HIPAA). Trustees and Beneficiaries must navigate these regulations carefully to access and advocate for the healthcare wishes of the incapacitated individual.

Practical Implications

1. Clarity and Communication: The inclusion of an AHD provides clear guidance to Trustees and Beneficiaries about the principal's healthcare wishes, reducing ambiguity and potential conflict in decision-making processes. This clarity ensures that healthcare decisions are made more efficiently and in alignment with the individual's preferences.

2. Coordination with Financial Decisions: Trustees often have control over financial aspects of the estate that can impact healthcare decisions, such as the allocation of funds for medical care. An AHD can guide Trustees in making financial decisions that support the healthcare preferences of the individual.

3. Impact on Beneficiaries: Beneficiaries may have emotional or financial interests in the healthcare decisions of the estate principal. An AHD serves as a critical tool in balancing these interests with the principal's wishes, ensuring that healthcare decisions are not unduly influenced by Beneficiaries' preferences or potential conflicts of interest.

The integration of an AHD into a Trust Centered Estate Plan is a nuanced process with profound legal and practical implications. Legally, it delineates clear authority and ensures compliance with State-specific regulations and healthcare laws. Practically, it provides clarity and guidance to Trustees and Beneficiaries, ensuring that healthcare decisions are made in accordance with the individual's wishes and are coordinated effectively with the financial management of the estate. For individuals planning their estate, understanding these implications is crucial to ensuring that their healthcare preferences are respected and upheld within the broader context of their estate planning goals.

State-Specific Statutes and Their Influence on Healthcare Directives: A Comparative Analysis

State-specific statutes significantly influence the creation, interpretation, and implementation of AHDs, DNRs and POLSTs. These laws provide the legal framework within which individuals can express their healthcare preferences and ensure they are respected.

State statutes dictate the requirements for drafting AHDs, DNRs and POLSTs, including the necessary content, format, and the process for making these documents legally binding. Individual State statutes outline specific provisions for AHDs, such as the appointment of an agent, the authority granted to this agent and the conditions under which the AHD becomes effective. These statutes ensure that the documents meet legal standards, promoting their enforceability and effectiveness in representing healthcare wishes.

The interpretation of AHDs, DNRs and POLSTs can vary significantly based on State laws, which provide guidelines on how healthcare providers and legal representatives should understand and act upon the wishes documented in these forms. State-specific statutes may define key terms and outline the scope of decision-making authority granted to healthcare agents, affecting how these documents are applied in clinical settings. This legal framework helps prevent misunderstandings and conflicts regarding patient care decisions.

State laws establish the mechanisms for enforcing AHDs, DNRs and POLSTs, detailing the legal obligations of healthcare providers and the rights of patients and their representatives. These statutes may include provisions for recognizing and honoring these documents across different healthcare settings, ensuring that patients' end-of-life care preferences are respected. Furthermore, State laws can prescribe penalties for failure to comply with the directives laid out in these documents, reinforcing their authority and effectiveness.

While State-specific statutes provide essential legal foundations for AHDs, DNRs and POLSTs, they also introduce challenges. The variability of laws across States can complicate the process for individuals who move between States or receive care in a State different from where their directive was created. Additionally, the evolving nature of healthcare laws necessitates continuous updates to these documents to ensure they remain compliant and reflective of current legal standards. It is important to note, while each State has specific laws governing these documents in their creation and use, most well-crafted documents will be honored across jurisdictional lines. AHDs specifically can be written to be clear enough to be effective in most jurisdictions.

State-specific statutes play a crucial role in shaping the drafting, interpretation, and enforcement of AHDs, DNRs and POLSTs. These laws ensure that these documents are created in a legally valid manner, interpreted correctly by healthcare providers and enforced in a way that respects individuals' healthcare preferences. Understanding the impact of these statutes is essential for individuals creating their healthcare directives, healthcare providers responsible for implementing them and legal professionals advising on estate and healthcare planning.

The integration of AHDs, DNRs and POLSTs into Trust Centered Estate Plans is a dynamic area, heavily influenced by evolving healthcare laws and patient rights. As legal practitioners and individuals navigate this landscape, several future considerations emerge, necessitating a forward-looking approach to estate and healthcare planning.

The digitization of healthcare records and legal

documents presents both opportunities and challenges. Future estate plans may increasingly incorporate digital versions of AHDs, DNRs and POLSTs, ensuring easy access for healthcare providers across various settings. However, this shift necessitates robust security measures to protect patient privacy and comply with regulations such as HIPAA. Legal practitioners must stay abreast of technological developments, integrating digital solutions that enhance accessibility while safeguarding sensitive information.

As individuals move across State lines, either during their lifetime or in seeking healthcare, the variability of laws governing AHDs, DNRs and POLSTs becomes a significant issue. Future legal frameworks may need to address the portability of these documents, ensuring that a directive valid in one State is recognized and enforceable in another. This consideration calls for a more unified approach to healthcare directives across jurisdictions, potentially involving federal legislation or interstate compacts. While laws differ, many lawyers have made it a practice to draft AHDs in a manner that makes them acceptable across State lines. DNRs and POLSTs are more problematic.

The evolution of healthcare paradigms, including increased emphasis on patient-centered care and autonomy, impacts the role and formulation of AHDs, DNRs and POLSTs. Future estate planning must consider these paradigms, ensuring that directives not only specify medical interventions but also reflect the individual's broader values and quality of life preferences. This shift may require developing more nuanced and flexible documents as well as ensuring that healthcare proxies are thoroughly educated on their healthcare laws and patient rights which are subject to legislative changes, influenced by societal attitudes, medical advancements and advocacy efforts. Legal practitioners and individuals must remain informed about potential changes to laws affecting AHDs, DNRs and POLSTs. Additionally, there is a growing role for advocacy, both in shaping future legislation to better accommodate patient needs and in educating the public about the importance of proactive healthcare planning.

As societies become increasingly diverse, estate plans incorporating AHDs, DNRs and POLSTs must reflect a broad range of cultural, religious and personal values. Future considerations include developing culturally sensitive approaches to end-of-life care planning and ensuring that legal instruments are adaptable to diverse belief systems. This diversity underscores the need for personalized, empathetic conversations between legal practitioners, healthcare providers and individuals as they navigate these complex decisions.

The future of integrating AHDs, DNRs and POLSTs into Trust Centered Estate Plans is marked by rapid advancements, shifting paradigms and an ever-evolving legal landscape. For individuals and legal practitioners, staying informed, advocating for patient rights and embracing technological and societal changes are crucial steps in ensuring that healthcare directives remain effective, respectful of patient autonomy and aligned with the broader goals of estate planning. This forward-looking approach will be essential in navigating the complexities of healthcare planning in the years to come, ensuring that individuals' wishes are honored in an increasingly complex healthcare environment.

Integrating Ethics, Technology, and Cultural Sensitivity into AHDs within Trust Centered Estate Planning

The creation of AHDs, alongside DNRs and POLSTs requires a careful consideration of legal, ethical and personal values. These documents are crucial components of a Trust Centered Estate Plan, acting as bridges between personal healthcare wishes and the legal framework that supports their execution. However, their effectiveness and adherence are subject to a variety of factors, from the role of Healthcare Proxies to the influence of cultural and religious beliefs.

Ethical considerations are paramount in the drafting. These documents often confront deeply personal and sometimes controversial issues, such as end-of-life care and the extent of life-sustaining treatments. It is essential for individuals, alongside their legal and healthcare advisors, to approach these directives with a sense of empathy, respect for autonomy and an understanding of the ethical dilemmas they may present. This includes acknowledging the Patient's right to decline treatment, the impact of such decisions on family members and Beneficiaries and the ethical obligations of healthcare providers to respect these choices.

Technological advancements have significantly impacted how AHDs, DNRs and POLSTs are created, stored and accessed. Digital record-keeping systems offer the potential for these crucial documents to be readily available to healthcare providers in emergency situations, ensuring that a Patient's healthcare wishes are respected without delay. However, this also raises concerns about privacy, data security and the need for standardized systems that can communicate across different healthcare platforms.

Ensuring that a Patient's wishes are followed requires a concerted effort from healthcare providers, legal professionals and family members. Education about the existence and importance of these directives is crucial, as is the establishment of clear protocols for accessing and interpreting these documents in urgent care settings. Misconceptions about the nature and purpose of AHDs, DNRs and POLSTs can hinder their effectiveness, making it vital for professionals to engage in open dialogues with patients and their families about what these documents entail and how they serve the Patient's best interests.

Cultural, religious and personal beliefs about death and dying deeply influence their creation. Recognizing and respecting these diverse perspectives is crucial in crafting documents that truly reflect the Patient's wishes. Legal and healthcare professionals must demonstrate cultural sensitivity and awareness, ensuring that directives are not only legally sound but also personally meaningful.

Finally, their enforcement in emergency situations presents a unique set of challenges. Healthcare providers often must make rapid decisions in high-stress environments. Establishing clear, accessible protocols for identifying and following these directives is essential to ensure that the Patient's end-of-life preferences are honored, even in the most urgent of circumstances.

These documents play a pivotal role in Trust Centered Estate Planning, serving as a testament to an individual's healthcare preferences and ethical values. The integration of these directives requires a multifaceted approach that considers legal obligations, ethical dilemmas, technological advancements and the rich tapestry of cultural and personal values. By addressing these considerations with sensitivity and respect, legal and healthcare professionals can ensure that these documents serve their intended purpose: to honor the healthcare wishes of individuals at the most critical moments of their lives.

The Intersect of Healthcare Directives and Estate Planning

As we conclude our discussion of AHDs, DNRs and POLSTs within the framework of Trust Centered Estate Plans, it's evident that these legal instruments are not merely administrative tools but profound expressions of individual autonomy and personal values. This Chapter has provided an analysis of the legal, practical and ethical considerations involved in integrating these healthcare directives into estate planning, offering valuable insights into their complexities and nuances.

It is critically important to understand State-specific statutes which impact the drafting, interpretation and enforcement of these directives. Respecting the legal landscape of each jurisdiction ensures that healthcare directives are both effective and enforceable.

Moreover, the evolving nature of healthcare laws and patient rights demands ongoing vigilance and adaptability from individuals and legal practitioners alike. The future considerations highlighted in this Chapter—ranging from technological advancements in digital healthcare records to the increasing emphasis on patient autonomy—suggest a landscape of estate planning that is both dynamic and challenging.

In navigating these complexities, we hoped to underscore the paramount importance of clear communication, informed decision-making and proactive planning. By integrating AHDs, DNRs and POLSTs into Trust Centered Estate Plans, individuals not only secure their healthcare wishes but also provide clarity and guidance to their loved ones and appointed agents, mitigating potential conflicts and ensuring that their values are honored. The integration of healthcare directives into estate planning is a multifaceted endeavor that requires careful consideration of legal principles, practical realities and ethical values. As healthcare laws and societal attitudes continue to evolve, so too will the strategies for incorporating these essential directives into comprehensive estate plans, ensuring that individual autonomy remains at the heart of healthcare and estate planning decisions.

"Discourage litigation."

—ABRAHAM LINCOLN

"The only happy litigants are those whose cases are yet to be heard."

—UNKNOWN TRIAL LAWYER

"I was never ruined but twice: once when I lost a lawsuit, and once when I won one."

—VOLTAIRE

"Avoid lawsuits beyond all things; they pervert your conscious, impair your health, and dissipate your property."

—JEAN DE LA BRUYERE

CHAPTER TWELVE

Trust Litigation

L iving Revocable Trusts stand as a testament to the desire for privacy, efficiency and control in estate planning, embodying the Trustor's intentions for the seamless transfer of their legacy. Yet, despite their structured flexibility and the foresight with which they are often crafted, these Trusts are not immune to disputes and challenges. The landscape of Trust litigation is complex, layered with nuanced legal principles and practical considerations that both Trust defenders and challengers navigate through. This Chapter looks at Trust disputes, touching on how these conflicts arise, the litigation process and the multifaceted outcomes that Courts may decree.

Beginning with an overview of the common grounds for challenging Living Revocable Trusts, we will discuss some aspects that may come under scrutiny—

ranging from the Trustor's mental capacity to allegations of undue influence, and the procedural validity of the Trust itself. Understanding these potential vulnerabilities is key to both preparing a robust defense and articulating a cogent challenge.

This Chapter outlines the procedural journey through the litigation process, from the initiation of a challenge, through discovery, motions that may preempt a trial, and ultimately, the Courtroom battles that decide the fate of the Trust. Special attention is given to the strategic stages of "Motions to Dismiss" and "Summary Judgment"—critical junctures that offer a pathway to resolve disputes efficiently and with lesser financial strain.

We will also look at the various outcomes of Trust litigation, providing clarity on how Courts adjudicate these matters and the implications of their decisions. From amendments and revocations to shifts in trusteeship and specific Court directives, the potential judicial remedies and adjustments underscore the importance of precision in Trust drafting and the adherence to fiduciary duties in Trust administration.

This Chapter aims to demystify the litigation process for non-lawyers while offering valuable insights for legal professionals grappling with Trust disputes. By understanding the dynamics at play, stakeholders can better navigate the complexities of Living Revocable Trusts, ensuring the Grantor's wishes are honored and the interests of Beneficiaries are safeguarded. Through this exploration, readers are equipped to appreciate the criticality of meticulous Trust formation, the potential for litigation and the strategic considerations vital for defending or challenging these pivotal estate planning instruments.

Types of Formal Challenges Against a Living Revocable Trust

Living Revocable Trusts are a cornerstone of modern estate planning, offering flexibility, privacy and a streamlined process for asset distribution upon the Grantor's passing. Despite their advantages, these Trusts are not immune to disputes and legal challenges. Understanding the common types of formal challenges can help in drafting more resilient Trusts and preparing for potential litigation. This section explores the most prevalent grounds on which a Living Revocable Trust might be contested.

One of the most common challenges to a Living Revocable Trust involves questioning the mental capacity of the Grantor at the time the Trust was created or amended. The legal requirement for creating a valid Trust includes the Grantor's ability to understand the nature of the Trust, the extent of their assets, the persons who are the natural Beneficiaries and the manner in which the Trust disposes of those assets. If it can be proven that the Grantor was suffering from dementia, Alzheimer's, or any other condition impairing their cognitive functions, the Trust's validity may be contested. This challenge often relies on medical records, witness testimony and expert opinions to substantiate claims of diminished capacity.

Another ground for challenging a Living Revocable Trust is undue influence, where it is alleged that the Grantor was subjected to pressure or manipulation by another individual, leading to decisions that do not reflect the Grantor's true intentions. This can be particularly difficult to prove, as it requires evidence that the Grantor's free Will was overridden by the influence of another, often a family member, caregiver or close associate. Indicators of undue influence include isolation of the Grantor, changes in the Grantor's behavior or estate plans that favor the influencer and the Grantor's dependency on the influencer.

Trusts must comply with specific State laws concerning their formation and execution. This includes proper signing, witnessing and notarization, as required by the jurisdiction where the Trust is established. Failure to adhere to these formalities can lead to a Trust being declared invalid. For instance, if the Trust document was not properly witnessed as required by State law, its validity can be challenged on the grounds that it does not meet the legal standards for a Trust agreement.

Challenges may also arise if there is suspicion that the Trust document, or amendments to it, were the result of fraud or forgery. This includes situations where the Grantor was deceived about the nature of the document they were signing or where the Grantor's signature was forged. Proving fraud or forgery involves demonstrating that deceit was employed to influence the Grantor's decisions or that the Grantor's signature was obtained without their knowledge or consent.

On rarer occasions, a Living Revocable Trust can be contested if its terms are contrary to public policy. This might include provisions that encourage divorce, discriminate based on race or religion or are deemed to be against the interests of public policy. While broad in interpretation, challenges on these grounds must clear a high threshold, as Courts are generally reluctant to invalidate Trust provisions based on public policy concerns unless they are clearly egregious.

Addressing these potential challenges when creating a Living Revocable Trust involves thorough planning, adherence to legal formalities and a clear understanding of the Grantor's wishes and mental state. Engaging experienced legal counsel can help ensure that a Trust is both compliant with State laws and reflective of the Grantor's true intentions, minimizing the risk of future litigation. Awareness of these common grounds for contestation is crucial for both legal practitioners and individuals involved in estate planning, offering a basis for more secure and dispute-resistant Trust arrangements.

Defending a Living Revocable Trust: The Initiation of Litigation Process

When a Living Revocable Trust is challenged, the defense's perspective and actions are pivotal in navigating the litigation process effectively. For those tasked with defending a Trust, whether Trustees, Beneficiaries or other interested parties, understanding the procedural landscape is crucial for mounting a robust defense. This section outlines the initial steps in the litigation process from the defense's standpoint, focusing on the formal response to the challenge, preparation for defense and the notification and involvement of interested parties.

The litigation process begins for the defending party upon receiving formal notice of the challenge against the Trust. This notice typically comes in the form of a Complaint or Petition filed by the challenging party in the Probate or Civil Court, alleging reasons for the Trust's invalidity or contesting its terms. The notification is a critical juncture, setting the stage for all subsequent defense activities. It triggers deadlines for the response and dictates the urgency of preparation.

Upon formal legal notification, the defending party must thoroughly understand the basis of the challenge. This involves a careful review of the Complaint's allegations, which might include claims of the Grantor's lack of mental capacity, undue influence, improper execution, fraud or that the Trust violates public policy. Recognizing the specific grounds of the challenge is essential for formulating an effective defense strategy.

The next step involves consulting with and engaging an attorney experienced in Trust and estate litigation. Legal counsel will assess the merits of the challenge, advise on the legal and practical aspects of defending the Trust and develop a strategy tailored to the specifics of the case. This strategy may include gathering evidence to counter the challenge, such as medical records, witness statements or documentation proving the Trust's proper execution.

The defense must prepare a formal response to the challenge known as an Answer, to be filed with the Court within a specified timeframe. This document counters the allegations made in the Complaint, addressing each point and asserting defenses based on law and fact. It may also raise procedural defenses, such as the challenger's lack of standing or the expiration of the statute of limitations. The answer sets the tone for the defense, signaling the basis upon which the Trust will be defended.

Defending a Trust is rarely a solitary endeavor. It often involves coordinating with other interested parties who have a stake in the Trust's outcome, such as co-Trustees, Beneficiaries or others named in the Trust document. Informing these parties about the challenge and aligning on a defense strategy is vital for a unified front. This may include joint legal representation or in some cases, separate counsel for different parties with distinct interests.

Defending against a challenge to a Living Revocable Trust requires a well-orchestrated approach from the moment the litigation is initiated. It demands quick, strategic actions beginning with understanding the challenge, engaging competent legal counsel, preparing a substantive response and coordinating with all interested parties. By meticulously addressing these steps, those defending a Trust can establish a solid foundation for their defense, aiming to uphold the Grantor's intentions and preserve the Trust's integrity.

Key Stages of Litigation in Trust Disputes

Litigation involving Trust disputes can be a complex and lengthy process, requiring a nuanced understanding of both legal principles and practical steps. This section breaks down the key stages of litigation, focusing on the pivotal moments which offer the opportunity to resolve the dispute efficiently and cost-effectively. By demystifying these stages, this explanation aims to provide clarity for non-lawyers and valuable insights for legal professionals navigating Trust litigation.

1. Motion to Dismiss

   A Motion to Dismiss is filed by the defendant early in the litigation process, arguing that the Complaint, even if true, does not provide a legal basis for the lawsuit to proceed. This stage is crucial because it seeks to terminate the litigation before the parties incur significant expenses in discovery and trial preparation. The grounds for a Motion to Dismiss in Trust disputes might include lack of jurisdiction, failure to state a claim upon which relief can be granted or expiration of the statute of limitations. If granted, the litigation ends at this point unless the plaintiff successfully appeals the decision or amends their Complaint to address the deficiencies identified by the Court.

2. Discovery

   Discovery is the initial and one of the most critical phases of litigation, where both parties exchange relevant information, documents and evidence related to the Trust dispute. This process allows each side to gather the facts, understand the opponent's arguments and prepare their case for trial. Discovery tools include interrogatories (written questions requiring written answers), depositions (sworn, out-of-court oral testimonies), requests for documents and requests for admissions (asking the other party to admit or deny specific statements). A properly conducted discovery can significantly influence the litigation's direction, enabling parties to build a strong case or identify grounds for early resolution through a Motion to Dismiss or Summary Judgment.

3. Summary Judgment

   Following discovery, either party may file a Motion for Summary Judgment, requesting the

Court to decide the case based on the evidence presented, without proceeding to a full trial. This motion asserts that there are no material facts in dispute and that the moving party is entitled to judgment as a matter of law. Summary Judgment is particularly appealing because it can significantly reduce litigation costs by avoiding the uncertainty and expense of a trial. Success at this stage requires demonstrating that the evidence unequivocally supports one party's version of the facts, making a trial unnecessary.

4. Pre-Trial Motions

Pre-trial motions are procedural or substantive requests made to the Court before the trial begins, addressing various issues such as the admissibility of evidence, the scope of the trial and other matters that can shape the trial's proceedings. These motions aim to streamline the trial process, clarify legal issues and in some cases, limit the issues or evidence that will be presented to the Jury or Judge.

5. Settlement Efforts

Throughout the litigation process but most commonly after the discovery phase and before the trial, parties may engage in settlement negotiations to resolve the dispute out of Court. Settlement can offer a less costly, more predictable and quicker resolution than a trial, allowing the parties to control the outcome directly. Mediation or arbitration may also be employed as alternative dispute resolution methods to facilitate a settlement.

6. Trial

If settlement efforts fail and the case is not resolved through motions, the dispute proceeds to trial, where each side presents its case to a Judge or Jury. The trial encompasses opening statements, witness testimonies, presentation of evidence, cross-examinations, and closing arguments. The trial's conclusion is marked by a verdict or judgment, determining the outcome of the dispute based on the merits of the case presented.

7. Appeals

Following the trial, the losing party may seek an appeal, challenging the trial Court's decision or the application of law. The appeals process involves a higher Court reviewing the trial Court's proceedings for legal errors that could have influenced the verdict. The outcome of an appeal can affirm, reverse or remand the case back to the trial Court for further proceedings.

Understanding the stages of litigation in Trust disputes provides individuals and legal professionals with a roadmap for navigating these complex cases. By strategically leveraging the Motion to Dismiss and Summary Judgment phases, parties can potentially resolve disputes efficiently and cost-effectively. Regardless of the path litigation takes, awareness of each stage's dynamics and implications is critical for effective case management and resolution strategy.

Resolving Disputes Over Living Revocable Trusts: Judicial Approaches and Outcomes

When litigation arises over Living Revocable Trusts, Courts employ a meticulous process to adjudicate disputes, considering the intricacies of Trust law and the specific circumstances of each case. This section explores how Courts resolve these disputes, the factors influencing their decisions and the range of possible Judicial outcomes, including amendments to the Trust, revocation, enforcement, financial compensation, changes in trusteeship and specific Court directives.

Determining the Validity of Challenges

The initial step in resolving a Trust dispute is determining the validity of the challenge. Courts examine the grounds of the challenge, such as allegations of the Grantor's lack of mental capacity, undue influence, fraud, improper execution or the Trust's contravention of public policy. Evidence is scrutinized closely, including medical records, witness testimony, document authenticity and compliance with legal formalities. The Court's determination hinges on whether the challenger can substantiate their claims with credible evidence.

Factors Considered in Rulings

In their rulings, Courts consider several key factors:
1. The Grantor's Intent:
   The primary goal is to ascertain and honor the Grantor's true intentions regarding the Trust and

its Beneficiaries.

2. The Legal and Factual Basis of the Challenge:
   Courts evaluate the legitimacy and strength of the evidence supporting the challenge.

3. The Impact on Beneficiaries:
   How the decision will affect current and future Beneficiaries is a significant consideration.

4. Statutory Requirements:
   Compliance with State laws governing Trust formation, amendment and revocation plays a crucial role.

Possible Judicial Outcomes

The Court's decision can lead to a variety of outcomes, depending on the nature of the dispute and the evidence presented:

1. Amendment of the Trust:
   If the Court finds that certain provisions of the Trust do not accurately reflect the Grantor's intentions due to factors like undue influence or errors, it may order amendments to those provisions to align with the Grantor's true wishes.

2. Revocation of the Trust:
   In cases where the Trust's creation was fundamentally flawed due to issues like lack of capacity or fraud, the Court may declare the entire Trust void. This revocation effectively resets estate distribution according to the Grantor's Will (if one exists) or

intestacy laws.

3. Enforcement of the Trust as Originally Written:
If the Court determines that the challenge lacks merit, it may enforce the Trust as initially drafted, affirming the Grantor's intent and the Trust's validity.

4. Financial Compensation:
The Court may order financial compensation to parties who have been wronged by actions related to the Trust's administration or by violations of the Trust terms. This can include restitution from individuals who unduly benefited at the expense of others.

5. Changes in Trusteeship:
If a Trustee is found to have acted in breach of their fiduciary duties, the Court can remove them and appoint a new Trustee. This change aims to ensure the Trust is managed in the best interests of the Beneficiaries going forward.

6. Specific Directives:
Courts can issue orders addressing specific issues raised during litigation, such as directives for how certain assets should be distributed or managed within the Trust framework.

Implications of Judicial Outcomes

The outcomes of Trust litigation have profound implications for all involved parties:

1. For Beneficiaries:
   Changes to the Trust can significantly impact Beneficiaries' entitlements and the timing of distributions. An adverse decision may also result in a Beneficiary receiving a reduced inheritance or being removed from the Trust altogether.
2. For Trustees:
   A ruling may affect a Trustee's authority or result in their removal and replacement. Trustees may also face personal financial liability if found to have breached their fiduciary duties.
3. For the Trust Administration:
   Judicial decisions can alter the Trust's administration, affecting its duration, asset management strategies and distribution plans. This may necessitate adjustments to comply with new Court orders or Trust provisions.

The Importance of Careful Trust Drafting and Administration

The range of possible outcomes in Trust litigation underscores the importance of meticulous Trust drafting and diligent administration. Careful drafting can minimize ambiguities and reduce the potential for disputes by clearly reflecting the Grantor's intentions and complying with legal requirements. Similarly, prudent administration, guided by the Trust's terms and fiduciary principles, can prevent mismanagement and breaches that could lead to litigation.

Understanding these potential outcomes highlights the seriousness of litigation and emphasizes the necessity for both Grantors and Trustees to seek experienced legal guidance in Trust creation and administration. Such foresight and diligence can significantly decrease the likelihood of disputes and ensure the Grantor's wishes are honored, protecting the interests of all parties involved.

Navigating the Complex Terrain of Living Revocable Trust Litigation

As we conclude our journey through the landscape of Living Revocable Trust litigation, it's evident that these legal instruments, while designed to provide clarity and peace of mind in estate planning, can become arenas of complex disputes. The discussions presented in this Chapter underscore the multifaceted nature of Trust disputes, highlighting the importance of a detailed understanding of both the legal framework and the practical dynamics involved in litigating such matters.

From the initiation of a challenge against a Trust based on questions of mental capacity, undue influence or procedural discrepancies, to the intricate procedures of the Court system including discovery, motions to dismiss and summary judgment and the trial process itself, we've explored the stages where litigation can pivot towards resolution or further contention. These early procedural stages, particularly motions to dismiss and for summary judgment, emerge as critical opportunities for parties to achieve a resolution without the financial and emotional toll of a full trial.

The potential outcomes of Trust litigation—ranging from the amendment or revocation of the Trust to changes in trusteeship and specific Court directives—demonstrate the Courts' flexibility in tailoring remedies to the unique circumstances of each case. These outcomes not only reflect the Courts' commitment to upholding the intent of the Grantor but also their consideration of the impact on Beneficiaries and the overall administration of the Trust.

This exploration serves as a reminder of the gravity of Trust disputes and the stakes involved for all parties. It reinforces the imperative for meticulous Trust drafting, the careful selection of Trustees and the vigilant administration of Trust duties. These steps are fundamental in minimizing ambiguities and potential conflicts, thereby safeguarding the Grantor's intent and the Trust's integrity. The next two Chapters, if understood and applied, will go a long way in avoiding Trust litigation.

For legal professionals, this Chapter provides a framework for navigating Trust litigation, offering strategic insights into managing disputes effectively. For non-lawyers, it demystifies the complexities of the process, emphasizing the importance of engaging experienced legal counsel when drafting, administering, or challenging a Living Revocable Trust.

Ultimately, the discussions herein underscore the significance of proactive estate planning and the critical role of legal guidance in ensuring that Living Revocable Trusts achieve their intended purpose. By appreciating the nuances of Trust litigation and embracing thorough preparation and strategic foresight, Grantors, Beneficiaries, and Trustees can better navigate the uncertainties of estate management, honoring the legacy and wishes of those who have planned for the future with care and consideration.

"To me, a lawyer is basically the person that knows the rules… We're all throwing the dice, playing the game, moving our pieces around the board, but if there is a problem, the lawyer is the only person who has read the rules of the game."

—JERRY SEINFIELD

"It's fine to celebrate success but it is more important to heed the lessons of failure."

—BILL GATES

"A bad lawyer is one who fails to spot problems, a good lawyer is one who perceives the difficulties, and the excellent lawyer is one who surmounts them."

—UNKNOWN

"Not only will you be sharing confidential information with this person, but you'll also be trusting their legal advice and ability to guide you through a situation you can't navigate alone."

—JASMINE ROY

CHAPTER THIRTEEN

Seasoned in the Crucible of Experience—The Monet Lawyer

We began this book with an introduction to the Monet metaphor. The Monet metaphor juxtaposed the talented, experienced and famous impressionist painter—a true artist even to those who did not find impressionist art to their liking, to a child who was just beginning her exploration into art. The comparison is unfair and perhaps a bit extreme in its application. Obviously a child, even one who would one day be world famous, has not had the opportunity to experience or even really begin to explore her native talent or the benefit of training and experience.

The purpose was not to focus on the child but rather to highlight the necessity of experience, training and talent of one who has become an accomplished artist. Monet's life as an artist is the ideal metaphor. He painted some 250 paintings of his lilies. He viewed the first 200 or so as unacceptable for public view. He labored for years to perfect his art and specifically to perfect his lilies. The point of the metaphor is to underscore that even for the talented, it takes time, great effort, training, and experiencing failure as well as success to bring even one subject to the heightened level desired.

Practicing law in a specific subject matter, just like medicine, architecture, engineering, construction, psychology, academia, piloting, even culinary arts, takes extraordinary experience, training and focus to be a specialist.

For example, in medicine, there exist at least twenty-four different boards that certify physicians in a variety of over 150 specialties. Engineering has Civil, Mechanical, Electrical, Chemical, Computer, Biomedical, Industrial, Environmental, etc. with over fifty specialties. In academia there are literally hundreds of areas of specialty. In law there is Criminal law, Civil law, Corporate law, Commercial law, Family law, Patent and Intellectual law, International law, Labor law, Constitutional law, Campaign law, Water law, Probate law, Estate Planning law, and many others. In the law, a lawyer cannot legally refer to themselves as a "specialist" unless they are certified or accredited by a Professional Legal Organization recognized by the

American Bar Association. This requires being a member of the Bar, a minimum number of years practicing in a specific specialty, peer review, evidence of expertise in the specialty, etc. If one is not certified or accredited as a specialist, the lawyer may only say his practice "focuses on" or "concentrates in" a certain area.

Before one engages a lawyer to represent them or to help them, wisdom would dictate that they be as careful with the selection as they would be in engaging a doctor or engineer. While a doctor could be highly educated and very intelligent with a pleasing bedside manner, their expertise, objective board and specialty certifications, training etc., should be examined. This is equally true before engaging a lawyer or any professional.

While a lawyer, any lawyer, is not a child as in our Monet metaphor, with no training or experience, there exist clear objective limits to every new lawyer. Of course, each lawyer is objectively intelligent—they were accepted to law school and passed the many requirements to graduate; they sat for the Bar, taking a comprehensive and rigorous multi-day exam. Law School is not easy—academically, emotionally, or even socially. Its objective is to train the mind of the student to "think like a lawyer," which is very different from other professions. The Law School experience lays a foundation for critical analysis, logical reasoning, problem solving, respect for another's point of view, attention to minute detail, persuasion, risk management, etc. But the experience is a foundation only. Oliver Wendell Holmes, Jr. said, "The life of the law has not been logic, it has been experience… the law embodies the story of a nation's development through many centuries and it cannot be dealt with as if it contained only the axioms and corollaries of a book of mathematics."

A graduate of Law School who then successfully sits for the Bar has only an entry-level grasp of the principles of the law and no experience in its practice. For all intents and purposes, they are a lawyer in name only. Probably the thing Law School instills most is best said by the famous Jurist, Learned Hand, "The spirit of liberty is the spirit which is not too sure that it is right. The spirit of liberty is the spirit which seeks to understand the minds of other men and women." Karl Llewellyn summed up thinking like a lawyer this way, "It is a compound of careful analysis of facts, careful checking of promises, logical control of conclusions, courage to follow your reasoning wherever it may lead and an ethical sense which gives one pause at the right places."

Law school and passing the Bar are wonderful but entry level just the same. Experience and failure as much as success will tutor and mentor a lawyer into a useful professional. Failure is like the heat of fire that makes metal malleable to be forged and pounded into shape to be useful. Experience is the metaphoric hammer.

Before engaging a lawyer, you should examine their

experience, their training, their failures, their successes, their certifications, their accolades. The combination of these many things will help you form a picture. Metaphorically ask yourself, is this the artist for whom I am looking?

Today you can turn to the Internet to begin the process of choosing a lawyer. Obviously you must be extremely careful. Not everything is of equal value on the Internet. If the lawyer has a website, peruse it. Are there online reviews? Again caution. Negative reviews are not fatal. Remember, you're trying to create a general picture. Anyone with experience has had some difficulties—reviews are not always accurate or honest. Is there a Wikipedia or other online source that will help you get a sense of the person?

Has the lawyer received any third-party recognition? Have they written or done any public or academic work? Are they recognized as a specialist or expert in Trust Centered Estate Planning? Do they offer or teach a class or seminar for professional or lay people on the subject? Do other lawyers or professionals refer their clients to them? Do they use them themselves?

Once you get a solid general feeling for the lawyer, their expertise and reputation, meet with them. The objective of the meeting is to make your final determination— is this the lawyer I want to create my Trust Centered Estate Plan? You have enough information now to create probing questions to help you make that determination. Let's discuss specifics that will propel you forward.

First, while you may actually know the answers to many of these questions, review them in some manner to verify you have the correct information. Please note, many people begin this process of the face-to-face meeting completely wrong. You are there to determine the quality of this lawyer, their experience, certifications, reputation, etc.—"Is this a Monet quality lawyer?" Yet, many people begin the interview by telling the lawyer about themselves, their estate planning needs, etc. While this is essential, it is not yet relevant until you determine to hire this lawyer. Begin by simply stating that you want to get to know each other and more particularly that you want to know about them. Have your questions ready. Then ask them, one by one. Keep in mind that this is a lawyer, so almost by definition, the lawyer will be able to talk well, be persuasive and articulate and deflect when it is in the lawyer's interests. Press on with confidence, ask your questions and ask again if necessary to get an answer you understand.

- How long have you been practicing law?
- How long have you been creating Trust Centered Estate Plans?
- Are there other areas of law which you practice?
- What percentage of your practice is focused on Trust Centered Estate planning?
- This should be easy for the lawyer because Errors

and Omissions malpractice insurance requires such a breakdown.

- Are there areas of law which you have practiced that have given you experience and made you a better Estate Planning lawyer?
- Have you ever participated in litigation that involves Estate Planning?
- Have any of the documents you have prepared ever been the subject of litigation?
- How many Trust Centered Estate Plans have you created?
- Have your Trust Centered Estate Plans been tested in the crucible of death – meaning have your clients' families had to rely on your work when your clients have died? About how many?
- Through the years of preparing Trust Centered Estate Plans have you changed the documents, have you refined and improved them? What motivated you to change them? Can you give me some examples?
- Have you reviewed other lawyers' Trust Centered Estate Plans? How do yours compare?
- Did you create your own Trust Centered Estate Plan, purchase it commercially, obtain it through continuing legal education, obtain it from a colleague or elsewhere?
- What kind of specific training have you had in estate planning, Trusts, Probate, etc.?
- Will you charge me a fee when I have questions

after we execute my Trust Centered Estate Plan?

- Will you charge me a fee to make changes to my Trust Centered Estate Plan?

- If you die, do you have a succession plan in place by which another lawyer of experience will honor the commitments to me that you will make?

- Without violating attorney/client privilege and speaking in general terms, have any Judges, lawyers, accountants, financial planners, etc. engaged your services to prepare their own Trust Centered Estate Plans. Please be specific as to the type of professional. Have they referred clients to you?

- Have you written and published on the subject of Trust Centered Estate Planning or other topics? Have you trained other professionals or lay people on this subject?

Be conversational in your interview; avoid being judgmental or critical. You are seeking to understand this lawyer and learn about their experience, reputation, skills and training. Certainly, never take an officious or superior attitude toward the lawyer. On their worst day, they are most probably much better equipped than you in the subject matter. By asking these questions, you will have gathered a great deal of information needed to help you determine whether or not their training, experience, temperament, reputation and skill has prepared this lawyer as the right one for you—a Monet quality lawyer.

Nevertheless, if you want to probe deeper you can easily formulate many more specific questions by reviewing Chapter Fourteen—The Monet Trust: Comprehensive and Simple. The focus of the Monet metaphor is not on the inexperience of the beginning artist but rather on the experience and ability of the Master artist. Like every professional you may engage in life, you want the best, you want a professional whose abilities have been forged in the hot furnace of failure and the hammer of experience, who will bring those abilities to bear in your service. You want a Monet lawyer!

"The difference between the almost right word and the right word is really a large matter—'tis the difference between the lightning bug and the lightning."
—MARK TWAIN (SAMUEL CLEMENTS)

"Words are…our most inexhaustible source of magic, capable of both inflicting injury and remedying it."
—J.K. ROWLING (DUMBLEDORE)

"He who wants to persuade should put his trust not in the right argument, but in the right word."
—JOSEPH CONRAD

"A word is not the same with one writer as with another. One tears it from his guts. The other pulls it out of his overcoat pocket."
—CHARLES PEGUY

CHAPTER FOURTEEN

Comprehensive and Simple—The Monet Trust

I n this Chapter, we ascend into the world of Revocable Living Trusts, exploring the multifaceted considerations that shape their drafting and administration. The Trust Centered Estate Plan is more than mere legal documents; it is carefully crafted instruments designed to protect assets, provide for loved ones, and ensure that a Grantor's wishes are honored both during their lifetime and after. If well done, it protects your legacy—the sweet, tender bonds of relationships and love.

In the last Chapter we revisited the Monet metaphor in discussing how to choose the right lawyer to draft your Trust Centered Estate Plan. In this Chapter, the Monet metaphor continues to be a help. We will examine some of the principles and some of the details that can make a Trust Centered Estate Plan a Monet quality plan. The three overall considerations to create a Monet quality Trust Centered Estate Plan are that the desires and objectives of the Grantor are incorporated fully: that the documents be comprehensive, and that the Plan be administratively simple.

Through an examination of these themes, this Chapter aims to provide a guide for drafting that is not only legally sound but also practically manageable. By weaving together legal principles and practical drafting strategies, we discuss creating Trusts that honor the Grantor's intentions, protect Beneficiaries' interests and ensure a lasting legacy.

Comprehensive

In the context of creating a Monet quality Trust Centered Estate Plan, "comprehensive" means providing for the future without knowing what the future may actually be. Let's discuss three examples of comprehensive provisions that will illuminate this principle: The age at which a Beneficiary may receive a distribution; the possibility that a designated Beneficiary may acquire a disability qualifying for government assistance; and how to protect the Trust from legal conflicts.

When considering the age at which Beneficiaries should gain control over the funds entrusted to them, several potential problems arise with allowing access too early. Young adults may not possess the necessary financial acumen or life experience to manage substantial assets or really any asset wisely. Impulsive spending, susceptibility to bad advice or investments in high-risk ventures could quickly deplete the Beneficiary's portion, negating the Grantor's intent to provide long-term security and support.

Establishing twenty-five as the minimum age for Beneficiaries to control their inheritance strikes a balance between allowing them time to mature and ensuring they are not overly restricted. By this age, many individuals have completed higher education, gained some life experience, and are better equipped to make informed financial decisions.

It is essential to clarify that, although the Beneficiary may not control the Trust assets directly until the age of twenty-five, the Trustee is authorized and encouraged to use the funds for the Beneficiary's benefit in the interim. This can include expenses related to education, healthcare, housing, and other support necessary for the Beneficiary's well-being and development. This approach ensures that the Beneficiary's needs are met while safeguarding the Trust's assets from unwise choices.

A point not to overlook is that it is not an uncommon occurrence that the intended Beneficiary predeceases the Grantor. This means that the person the Grantor intended to receive the distribution died before the Grantor. The Trust of course will have provided for such a possibility because it is comprehensive and will have named a contingent Beneficiary. That contingent Beneficiary may be under twenty-five. This will require provision in drafting the Trust.

Beneficiaries with disabilities who at the time of the intended distribution are on certain government assistance such as Supplemental Security Income (SSI) have specific protections available through the Omnibus Budget Reconciliation Act of 1993 (OBRA '93) and its progeny of laws. OBRA '93 allows Beneficiaries with disabilities to benefit from Trust assets without losing eligibility for crucial government benefits.

OBRA '93 permits the creation of both self-settled (or first party) Trusts, funded with the Beneficiary's assets, and third-party Trusts, funded by someone else, for example the Grantor of a Trust. This distinction is crucial for compliance and planning. The legislation mandates that Trust assets must supplement government benefits, not replace them. This allows for expenses not covered by government programs to be addressed by the Trust.

Self-settled Special Needs Trusts are required to have a payback provision to reimburse Medicaid benefits upon the Beneficiary's death, a requirement not applicable to third-party Special Needs Trusts.

Incorporating a Special Needs Trust within a Revocable Living Trust under OBRA '93 guidelines involves strategic drafting to ensure the Trust serves the Beneficiary's supplemental needs while adhering to legal standards.

The Trust must define supplemental needs clearly, grant the Trustee broad discretion for distributions, and for self-settled Trusts, include the mandatory payback provision.

For Beneficiaries with disabilities or special needs, incorporating a Special Needs Trust within the Revocable Living Trust is critical. This enables the Beneficiary to receive Trust distributions without disqualifying them from government assistance programs like Medicaid or Supplemental Security Income (SSI).

Granting the Trustee discretionary power to make distributions for the benefit of a special needs Beneficiary with disabilities ensures that the Trustee can provide for the Beneficiary's needs without jeopardizing their eligibility for public benefits. This protection has been available for over thirty years, yet most Trusts created today continue to make no provision for taking advantage of this crucial law. Therefore, most Trusts today fail to be "comprehensive" in this critical provision.

Almost every Will has some type of Non-Contest provision. Interestingly, most Trusts do not. Often, Clients will ask their lawyer to, "put that one-dollar thing in the Trust if someone contests it." The experienced lawyer will understand that the Client is asking for a Non-Contest provision. But the experienced lawyer will already have included an artfully written Non-Contest provision in both the Trust and the Pour-Over Will. Further, the artfully drafted Trust will have several other provisions that will deter contests.

Nevertheless, the "Non-Contest" clause itself is the main citadel protecting the Trust from formal attack. The best clauses are written by lawyers who have spent significant time in Court. These lawyers write Trusts from that perspective. They are not merely familiar with the process but are keenly aware of the dynamics, rules and nuances of litigation. Chapter Twelve of this book provides an overview of the litigation process. Every Trial Lawyer understands that contracts, including Trusts, are written for that forum— the Courtroom. The nuances of the Contract can open or shut the door to success in litigation.

There are basic legal principles on which the Court relies to interpret Trusts. One of those principles is to use the plain meaning of the words in the Trust. Sometimes there are "terms of art" used in the Trust which have meaning that have been long established through use, custom and Court interpretation that may supplant the ordinary usage. It takes an experienced lawyer to use language to the advantage of the client. The words of the Trust mean everything.

Often when a particular word, phrase or provision simply does not lend itself to such interpretation, the Court will try to determine the intent of the Grantor. This is the arena when the matter can be won or lost on the well-crafted and well-used choice of words. For example, below is the first few lines of a well-written Non-Contest clause:

No person, or entity, whether related to Grantors or not, has any claim of right to any distribution, bequest, inheritance or other except as stated herein. It is not the purpose of this Trust Agreement to be equitable or fair or to give any Beneficiary, other than Grantors, any deference or any opportunity, whatsoever, to dispute or raise any issue of any kind in relation to this Trust Agreement. It is Grantors' specific intent to foreclose any such ability or opportunity. If any person or entity claims that Grantors, or either of them, made any promise or any statement, in writing or otherwise, other than stated herein in relationship to any distribution, bequest, inheritance or other or that may be the basis or used as evidence for or to any claim of right other than stated herein, Grantors hereby revoke such statement or promise.

Litigation, especially the part that actually comes before the Judge, is not binary. It is not one thing or another thing. Because the arguments made to the Judge are often manifold, multiple, and because the lawyers may draw on numerous principles of law to persuade the Judge or upon which he will rely, one never really knows what argument will prevail. Therefore, a well-written Non-Contest clause, as well as the entire Trust Centered Estate Plan, should have numerous provisions to present to the Court in hopes of strengthening the documents and protecting the Grantor and Beneficiaries.

The above example of an addition to a Non-Contest clause is really written to the Judge and to the lawyers who may be presenting a potential adversary. Each sentence in various ways communicates that no one, including the Judge, should substitute their intent for the Grantor's intent. It states plainly and subtly, "I know what I am doing; I am doing what I intended to do; do not interfere." Judges are always looking for evidence of the Grantor's intent. Where the Grantor is concerned about a specific person who may cause problems, that person's name could be added to the Non-Contest provision; for example, "This provision shall apply specifically to John Doe, as well as others generally."

This type of language may appear not only in a Non-Contest provision, but under several headings and in several places in the Trust. Redundancy with such a precaution is not a vice.

We have taken a little bit of a deeper dive into three areas to illustrate the concept of providing for the future without knowing what the future will actually be. There are many additional areas in a well-written Trust, a Monet quality Trust, that will be comprehensive, for example:

- Naming the Trust and making specific reference to any previous Trust Agreement or specific reference that there might exist a previous Trust.
- The naming of Successor Trustees, including

the possibility that a Trustee could become incapacitated, or the possibility that all the named Trustees could fail, and the process for naming a successor in that case.

- Whether or not the Trust is revocable or amendable and the process to do so.

- Nearly every jurisdiction, every State, allows a contract/Trust to elect what State law will be used to govern and construe the document. This ability allows the Grantor to choose a State that may have laws more favorable to Trusts than the actual State in which the Trust is created. This is incredibly helpful and important. Some States have more favorable laws than other States. This ability is called "Choice of Law." For example, Delaware has very favorable laws for Corporations and Limited Liability Companies. More than sixty percent of Fortune 500 Companies use Delaware law. This ability to choose can be a benefit to your Trust Centered Estate Plan.

- The after-born or adopted children precaution, while not common, does come into play. This provides that if a child is born or adopted after the execution of the Trust, the provisions of the Trust may apply to such a person. Most Grantors think such a clause is unnecessary but may not consider generalities after execution.

- A provision in which the Grantor reserves to

themself specific rights, authority and power.

- Many provisions are broadly written to enable the Trustee to accomplish the things seen and unforeseen that may need to be done in the administration of the Trust.

- While Grantor's desires in the distribution of Trust assets must be clearly stated, there are unforeseen circumstances that ought to be addressed to provide for full compliance with the Grantor's desires.

- Provision should be made to protect Trust assets from creditors of Beneficiaries or from Beneficiaries themselves who try to encumber Trust assets before those assets are distributed to them.

- One of the most important provisions falls under the general idea of "accounting." The Trustee's obligation to account for their labors and Trust assets can be a door that allows adversaries to attack the Trust. This may be the single most used "point of the sword" to attack Trusts and Trustees. This is also where the experience, training and ability of the Monet-quality lawyer really come into play. While the accounting clause may be the easiest means for adversaries to access the Trust, in other words, the weakest place in the Trust's armor, the lawyer can make it the strongest. This will depend not only on the lawyer's skills but also on the choice of law referred to above.

- The Choice of Law provision may seem like enough to determine the authority and power of the Trustee because State law will have a statutory provision enumerating the Trustee's authority and power. But the wise lawyer will also state in the Trust document the details of the Trustee's authority and power. Again, this seems redundant but may prove essential to future circumstances.

- Earlier we discussed the idea that the Court will use the plain meaning of words or acknowledge the use of "terms of art," those terms clearly established by custom and usage over long periods of time. But wisdom dictates that specific terms should be defined in the document to avoid opportunity for challenge.

- Often the Grantors will make no provision for their funeral. Those who would be legally empowered to do so may no longer be in the close circle of the Grantors—they may be estranged family members. Therefore, wisdom would dictate that the Trustee or another be given that authority.

There are, of course, many other areas, some quite subtle, that the principle of "comprehensive" will be found. Providing for the future without knowing what the future will bring is essential in creating a Monet quality Trust—a Trust Centered Estate Plan that will protect the legacy of the Grantor and their loved ones.

Let us now turn our attention to creating a Trust Centered Estate Plan that is administratively simple. While every Trust Centered Estate Plan may feel complicated and impossible to understand, the reality is a well-written plan, intended to be administered with greater ease, will be administratively simple. There is a difference between complicated and complex. Complex means made up of different parts. A Trust Centered Estate Plan has at least six separate documents, all of which have several parts. The key is to take them individually, not all at once. Again, the concept is for the plan to be administratively simple for the Grantor and for the Grantor's family after the Grantor has passed.

The first place to look for administrative simplicity will be the Table of Contents. This will help you understand that your Trust Centered Estate Plan contains several distinct documents.

The second place to look for administrative simplicity is the Instructions. Every well-written plan will have step-by-step Instructions for the client. These Instructions will have a check list of tasks to perform by the client. The Instructions will cover everything from acquiring new real estate to dealing with financial institutions; from what to do with vehicles to personal property generally. It will include specific guidance on using the Durable Power of Attorney because financial institutions can be very difficult to work with. The Instructions will be thorough but not overwhelming. A really good lawyer will also highlight especially important portions to make it even simpler to understand.

There will be separate Instructions for the Successor Trustee once the Grantor has passed. Each of the documents will be found under its own section. Each document will have been carefully written to carry out the desires of the Grantor; each will be comprehensive; each will have provisions that will be helpful to the administrative process. For example, in the Trust itself there may be a specific provision about the tax treatment of the Trust before the Grantor's death and tax treatment after the Grantor's death. There will be a document titled, "Certificate of Trust." This will facilitate the Grantor's ability to work with financial institutions and title agencies without the need to copy the entire Trust. The Durable Power of Attorney may have a Notice on its face directed to financial institutions that they, the financial institution, should be very careful before they reject the document because they may be liable for the costs of rejection. This has been a wonderful warning to add since the crash of 2008—financial institutions routinely have made things more difficult for customers using Powers of Attorney. This Notice balances the power back in the Grantor's favor.

Drafting the Trust document with clear, concise language minimizes ambiguity and reduces the administrative burden. Avoiding legal jargon where possible and opting for straightforward descriptions of the Trust's mechanisms make it more accessible for Trustees and Beneficiaries alike.

Organizing the Trust Centered Estate Plan in a logical, intuitive format is helpful. This includes grouping related provisions together, using headings and subheadings for easy navigation and providing an accessible and simple table of contents. Such an organization helps Trustees quickly find the information they need without sifting through unrelated material.

Granting Trustees broad discretion in managing the Trust, in making distributions and in responding to Beneficiaries' needs will simplify administration. This allows Trustees to adapt to changing circumstances without Court intervention.

Specifying the ability for Trustees to consult with professional advisors (financial, legal, tax) can ensure that the Trust is managed with the requisite level of expertise. This can relieve Trustees of the burden of being experts in every aspect of Trust Administration.

Drafting a Trust Centered Estate Plan that combines provisions that make the documents comprehensive with administrative simplicity requires careful attention to structure, language and the inclusion of flexible and anticipatory provisions. By employing these principles, it is possible to create a Trust Centered Estate Plan that is both robust in its protections and manageable for those charged with its administration. This approach ensures that the Trust Centered Estate Plan is dynamic and effective in carrying out the Grantor's wishes, adaptable to the changing landscapes of law, family circumstances and Beneficiaries' needs, without becoming an unwieldy burden for Trustees.

As we conclude this Chapter and this book, it becomes clear that the creation of the Trust Centered Estate Plan is both a science and an art. In the end, the true measure of whether or not a Trust Centered Estate Plan is of Monet quality is whether or not it will accomplish the purpose for which it is created. Will it provide for the future without knowing what the future will bring—is it comprehensive? Will it be simple to administer while the Grantor is living and for the Trustee when the Grantor is gone? If the Trust Centered Estate Plan fully captures the intent of the Grantor, if it provides well for future contingencies, if it is simple in its administrative demands, it will be a work of art worthy of both confidence and admiration.

"You could leave life right now. Let that determine what you do and say and think."
—MARCUS AURELIUS

"The trouble is, you think you have time."
—BUDDHA

"Prepare for what is difficult while it is easy, do what is great while it is small."
—SUN TZU

"Inaction breeds doubt and fear...If you want to conquer fear... get busy."
—DALE CARNEGIE

"Procrastination is the thief of time, collar him."
—CHARLES DICKENS

CONCLUSION

The Mayflower Moving Truck Principle

In this book we have taken a journey to examine the essence of legacy and the need for expert estate planning to preserve the true riches of family and shared experiences. The imagery of Modern Grave Robbers, representing the failure to plan effectively, has been discussed as a warning of the repercussions that inadequate preparation can have on your family's most cherished assets—tender loving memories and bonds.

As we strolled through the landscape of estate planning, our pace and anxiety quickened as it became evident that the impact of Modern Grave Robbers extends far beyond financial implications. They steal time, choice, privacy and peace, disrupting the very fabric of your family's well-being and unity. It is in acknowledging these profound losses that we are compelled to take decisive action in fortifying our family's legacy against the uncertainties of life.

The Mayflower Moving Truck Principle stands as a poignant reminder of the unpredictability of life and death, highlighting the sobering reality that many individuals depart from this world unexpectedly, leaving their loved ones vulnerable and unprepared. The stories of families who have experienced the sudden loss of a loved one without proper legal preparation weave a tapestry of heartache, resilience and the enduring power of family bonds.

Ann and Michael Johnson, a young couple full of dreams and aspirations, had meticulously planned for their future together. Tragically, a fatal car accident cut their lives short, leaving their two children orphaned and adrift in a sea of uncertainty. Such a death occurs every twelve minutes in this country. Without any formal plan in place, the children's guardianship and inheritance became entangled in a legal web, amplifying their grief and isolation. The lack of preparation not only robbed the children of their parents but also of their stability, security and sense of belonging. The family faced prolonged legal battles, financial instability and emotional turmoil, all of which could have been avoided with proper planning. Unrealized by the extended family, the guardians eventually appointed by the Court or even the children, a serious wrinkle will emerge when the first child turns eighteen. He will get control of his portion of their parents' estate including life insurance proceeds, a potentially devastating burden for an eighteen-year-old.

John Simmons, a pillar of his community and a devoted family man, believed he had time on his side to create an estate plan. However, a sudden heart attack shattered that illusion, leaving his family grappling with the aftermath of his demise. Unexpected death from cardiovascular disease takes someone every forty seconds. The absence of a clear plan led to financial turmoil, emotional upheaval and a fractured sense of security for his loved ones. The chaos and confusion that ensued in the absence of proper legal preparation not only jeopardized the family's financial well-being but also strained their emotional resilience and unity. The family faced mounting debts, legal disputes and uncertainty about their future, all of which could have been prevented with timely planning.

Maria Martinez, a compassionate soul who lived for her family, passed away when she was reaching for something in her garage and a can of paint fell on her head. Every three minutes and twenty-one seconds someone dies unexpectedly from an accident in their home. Her children, already reeling from the loss and strange death of their mother, found themselves embroiled in disagreements over her estate, straining the very bonds that Maria had worked so hard to nurture.

The lack of clarity and legal documentation not only fueled conflicts among family members but also eroded the peace and harmony that Maria had cherished and nurtured within her family. The family endured bitter disputes, fractured relationships and emotional distress, all stemming from the absence of a clear estate plan that could have preserved their unity and peace.

Soseti and Alana Thompson, a couple deeply in love and brimming with hope, never fathomed the tragedy that would befall them. A devastating fire claimed their lives, leaving their infant son as the last vestige of their union. Every two hours and twenty-four minutes someone dies in a fire. In the absence of a plan, the baby's custody and future hung in limbo, a stark reminder of the fragility of life's tapestry. The failure to prepare legally not only left the child's future uncertain but also plunged the extended family into a legal battle, draining them emotionally and financially as they struggled to navigate the aftermath of the tragedy. The family faced custody disputes, financial hardship, and emotional trauma, all of which could have been mitigated with proper estate planning.

The Reynolds siblings, bound by love and shared memories, faced the ultimate test of their family ties when their parents passed away in quick succession. Unprepared for the complexities that assaulted them, they were confronted with wave after wave of difficult decisions, each one laden with emotional weight and family implications. The lack of legal preparation not only delayed the resolution of their parents' affairs but also strained their own relationship and unity. The family endured prolonged legal battles, emotional strain and fractured bonds, all of which could have been avoided with proactive planning.

These illustrations give us a glimpse of the hurt that failure to plan may cause. Each story serves as a testament to the importance of proactive estate planning, not just as a legal obligation but as a profound act of love and protection for those we hold dear.

The reality is that without proper legal preparation, families are left vulnerable to the merciless whims of fate or the hunger of avarice—Modern Grave Robbers. The anguish, chaos, and heartbreak that unfolds in the wake of unanticipated tragedies can serve as cautionary beacons, illuminating the serious consequences of neglecting to safeguard one's legacy.

Perhaps you stand at the crossroads of decision. Is your family, your legacy, protected? The Mayflower Moving Truck Principle—the idea that we have no idea when we will die—reminds us to be wise, to prepare. The alternative is unnecessary and can so easily be avoided.

ACKNOWLEDGEMENTS

Nearly forty years of working very closely with individuals and families in the legal arena have schooled me and motivated me to write this book. I am grateful to each one. My first mentor in the subject was Daniel W. Malcum, a supremely good lawyer and well-skilled in complex estate planning. He took no prisoners when it came to his demands on this young associate lawyer. The years that I spent under his intense tutorage have benefitted thousands of my clients.

I express special and heartfelt thanks to my son and business partner, John Hawkins. He has endured years of my seemingly constant drive to create the best possible law practice that will be a benefit to our clients. He has added to my efforts with his patient wisdom and skillful applications to create such a practice. I am deeply grateful.

I am grateful to my typist for the efforts on numerous early drafts—Dorothy Openshaw. I am, as always, indebted to Marci Andrews Wahlquist for her excellent editing skills. I always think that after so many drafts I have arrived at perfection. Then she applies her incredible intellect and experience, and I am always amazed. Thank you, Marci. I am also grateful for the labor of love that Susette van der Beek-Afu, my sister-in-law and a highly skilled legal secretary, gave in reading and critiquing early drafts. Her wisdom, common sense and editing skill were an extraordinary gift.

College and law school were often very intense. At times I thought I would never forget the professors. Most of them I have forgotten. Yet, a few are engraven on my psyche. Thank you to Alma Don Sorensen, Louis C. Midgley, Edward Firmage, Kristine Strachan, Thomas Lund, Bill Lockhart and Donna Lee Bowen. They raised me from ignorance to having some sense of knowledge and ability to reason.

Thank you to the many lawyers who have provided that most intense and unique of all "peer" review via our adversary legal system. Each in their own way has made me a better lawyer, a better writer, a better advocate and a much better human being. Special thanks to my former law partner, Lonn Litchfield. Through many years of trial practice and helping clients legally prepare for death he is as much responsible for what I do today as I am.

The kind but challenging impositions of countless Judges over decades of Court appearances is what gave me the insights to develop the best possible approach to avoid litigation. Each deserves acknowledgment but special thanks to Federal Judges David K. Winder, Bruce S. Jenkins and David Sam and State Judges Robert Hilder, Christine M. Durham, Matthew B. Durrant, Lynn W. Davis, Joseph W. Anderson, Sandra Peuler, Tyrone E. Medley and Judith S.H. Atherton. Although every judge I appeared before added to my experience, ability and wisdom, with each of these I had extended experience and they went out of their way to make me a better lawyer and a much better human being.

I am the most grateful for and want to acknowledge each of my life changing and character-building children. Author Ernestine Gilbreth Carey said that she had "only twelve children" but her husband Frank Bunker Gilbreth, Jr. said that he had "twelve only children." This is how I feel. Each of my children is to me an only child. My wife, the former Arlene van der Beek, is the center focus of my love and gratitude. She has provided countless hours of logistical support for this book. But more importantly she has added immeasurably to my well-being, happiness and joy.

I do not have the vocabulary or ability to express the depth and breadth of the gratitude I feel to Him to whom I owe all gratitude.

ABOUT THE AUTHOR

Gregory P. Hawkins is a nationally recognized attorney, author, and speaker with over 40 years of experience in trust law and estate planning. As a lawyer and an Accredited Estate Planner he has helped thousands of families protect their wealth, avoid costly legal battles, and secure their legacies through his Trust Centered Estate Planning method.

With decades of courtroom experience, Hawkins has seen firsthand the devastating consequences of poor estate planning—family disputes, unnecessary litigation, avoidable taxes and the high cost of probate. Avoiding the courtroom has provided the quintessential approach empowering families to escape these pitfalls, ensure a seamless transfer of wealth, reduce stress, and achieve lasting peace.

Tens of thousands have attended his live seminars, where he breaks down estate planning with clarity, real-world strategies, and expert insights. Thousands more have entrusted him with their estate planning needs. But the ultimate proof of his method's effectiveness isn't in theory.

Countless families have relied on his approach at the most critical moment—the passing of a loved one. Time and again, his method has delivered exactly what it was designed to: clarity in uncertainty, protection in vulnerability, and peace when it mattered most.

Hawkins's work isn't just about preparing documents—it's about protecting families, preserving legacies, and ensuring that the right plan actually works when it's needed most.

Beyond his legal expertise, Hawkins is a respected public speaker, professional educator, and former elected official. He has authored multiple books and articles on law, ethics, and public policy, reflecting his deep commitment to empowering individuals and families with the knowledge they need to make informed decisions.

In Truth About The Living Trust, Hawkins pulls back the curtain on the estate planning industry, exposing common myths and costly pitfalls while delivering clear, actionable steps to help readers protect their assets, minimize taxes, and avoid probate nightmares. Whether you're starting your estate plan or refining an existing one, this book provides the clarity, confidence, and strategy to take control of your legacy—before it's too late.